Jesus: Author and Finisher

JESUS
AUTHOR AND FINISHER

MORRIS H. CHAPMAN

Compiler

BROADMAN PRESS
Nashville, Tennessee

Unless otherwise stated, all Scripture quotations are from the King James Version of the Bible. Scripture quotations marked NASB are from the *New American Standard Bible*. Copyright © The Lockman Foundation, 1960, 1962, 1963, 1971, 1972, 1973, 1975, 1977. Used by permission.

Library of Congress Cataloging-in-Publication Data

Jesus, author and finisher.

Fourteen sermons preached at the Southern Baptist Convention 1986 Pastors' Conference in Atlanta.
1. Jesus Christ—Person and offices—Sermons.
2. Southern Baptist Convention—Sermons. 3. Baptists—Sermons. 4. Sermons, American. I. Chapman, Morris.
II. Southern Baptist Convention. Pastors' Conference (1986 : Atlanta, Ga.)
BT202.J4255 1987   232   87–6387
ISBN 0-8054-5047-5 (pbk.)

With genuine love and appreciation to
the members of the Sanctuary Choir of
First Baptist Church, Wichita Falls, Texas,
for their participation in the 1986 Pastors'
Conference in Atlanta, Georgia. Their songs
of praise and adoration led us to "look unto
Jesus, the author and finisher of our faith."

Contents

Foreword

The publication of the sermons preached at the Southern Baptist Convention 1986 Pastors' Conference in Atlanta would not have been accomplished except for the spiritual sensitivity of those in positions of responsibility at Broadman Press. An understandable hesitation initially prevailed. Questions like, "Would the publication of this compilation set a precedent for future pre-convention conferences?" had to be carefully and prayerfully considered. The decision to proceed with this project seemed to rest finally on the fact that the principle focus of Southern Baptists has been and must always be Jesus. These messages were preached and are published sequentially presenting the Personhood of Jesus from preexistence to preeminence. The editors graciously invited the compiler to provide a sermon for the beginning chapter.

I am grateful to Broadman for polishing our preaching for publication. In the process they have cautiously sustained the substance of the sermons. My secretary, Barbara Schaefer, not only transcribed the messages from cassette tapes, she retyped them following a first editing by the compiler. I am most appreciative to her for the extra hours and extraordinary effort which were gladly given.

I am likewise grateful to two of my hardworking Pastors' Conference colleagues for their invaluable input and encouragement: Ned Matthews, Conference Vice-President and Pastor of Parkwood Baptist Church, Gastonia, North Carolina; and Dwight "Ike" Reighard, Conference Secretary-Treasurer and Pastor of New Hope Baptist Church, Fayetteville, Georgia.

During the eight years I have served as Pastor of the First Baptist Church, Wichita Falls, I have grown in so many ways, thanks to the love and patience of her people. They greatly deserve my sincerest gratitude for their support and encouragement especially during the year I served as President of the Pastors' Conference.

I have no greater friend on earth than my dear wife, Jodi. I love her deeply and I am grateful for her love for me. Through the years I have discovered that her spiritual discernment is amazingly accurate. As you would imagine, I listen closely to her valued counsel. Her contribution to my life and ministry is so vast as to be immeasurable.

I thank God for all who have taught me more about Jesus. I'm glad God called me to preach and that He has allowed me the privilege of having innumerable friends among my fellow pastors.

Morris H. Chapman

Introduction

The inquiring minds of men came to Philip saying, "Sir, we would see Jesus" (John 12:21). Philip told Andrew and again both Andrew and Philip told Jesus. Upon hearing their request, Jesus answered, saying, "The hour is come, that the Son of Man should be glorified" (John 12:23). As God prepared my heart for planning the Southern Baptist Convention Pastors' Conference in Atlanta, 1986, He strongly impressed upon me to ask every preacher simply to preach Jesus. With increasing intensity I was convicted and convinced that we should follow the pattern of Philip when he encountered the eunuch. The Bible says, "Then Philip . . . preached unto him Jesus" (Acts 8:35).

The men who were invited to preach on the program of the Pastors' Conference graciously consented to accept specific assignments in preaching the Personhood of Jesus from preexistence (Col. 1:15-17) to preeminence (Col. 1:18-19). For two days in Atlanta I listened to them preach and I praised the Lord. Like Paul they "determined not to know any thing among you, save Jesus Christ" (1 Cor. 2:2). One by one they mounted the platform preaching "not with enticing words of man's wisdom, but in demonstration of the Spirit and of power" (1 Cor. 2:4). Their power for that hour in Atlanta was like the prophets of old who thundered "Thus saith the Lord!"

I could see it on their faces. I could hear it in their voices. I could sense it about their spirits. They were prepared to preach the Lord Jesus Christ, God's Living Word. Surely the sermons in this volume were prepared with the prayer of David on the hearts of the men who preached them, "Let the words of my mouth and the meditation of my heart, be acceptable in thy sight, O Lord, my strength and my redeemer" (Ps. 19:14).

Our Lord Jesus said, "I am the Alpha and Omega, the beginning and the ending, . . . which is, and which was, and which is to come, the Almighty" (Rev. 1:8). Jesus is saying, "I am the First and the Last." Alpha is the first letter of the Greek alphabet. Omega is the last letter of the Greek alphabet. Jesus is saying, "I am the A and the Z." In reality He is saying, "I am the A, the Z, and all the letters from A to Z." In fact, Jesus is not only the letters, He is the language. He is the Way, the Truth and the Life (see John 14:6). In Jesus we have all of God. All things were created by Him (see Col. 1:16). All things are controlled by Him (see Heb. 1:3). All things will be consummated by Him (see Eph. 1:10). When we see Jesus, we see God, the Almighty. When we see Jesus, we see the "image of the invisible God" (Col. 1:15). From the first words of Genesis to the last words of Revelation, we see Jesus!

The Bible says, "And thou shalt call His Name Jesus" (Matt. 1:21). He is called Wonderful, Counselor, The mighty God, The everlasting Father, The Prince of Peace (see Isa. 9:6). He is the Light of the World (see John 8:12), the Dayspring (see Luke 1:78), the Bright and Morning Star (see Rev. 22:16). He is the Lamb of God (see John 1:29) and the Lord God Almighty (see Rev. 15:3). Jesus is Savior (see Acts 13:23) and chief Shepherd (see 1 Pet. 5:4). To the builder He is the Chief

Cornerstone. To the baker He is the Living Bread. To the gardener He is the Rose of Sharon and the Lily of the Valley. To the farmer He is the Sower. To the geologist He is the Rock of Ages.

I am saying Jesus is "the King of Kings and Lord of Lords" (1 Tim. 6:15). He is Lord above the earth, on the earth, and beneath the earth. "At the Name of Jesus every knee should bow . . . and that every tongue should confess that Jesus Christ is Lord, to the glory of God the Father" (Phil. 2:10-11, KJV).

Several years ago I preached a sermon from Hebrews 12:1-2 entitled "Run for the Finisher." Since that time the phrase "Looking unto Jesus the author and finisher of our faith" has reminded me repeatedly that we are to set our "affection on things above, not on things on the earth" (Col. 3:2). I long to look unto Jesus and none other for my source of strength. Sometimes I fail, but He never fails me. Sometimes I fall, but He has never forsaken me. I thank God that His grace is sufficient. We have a race to run, but we run not for the finish, we run for the Finisher! When we grow weary in the race, Jesus has promised rest. His great invitation recorded in Matthew 11:28-30 is an invitation to rest. He said,

> Come unto me, all ye that labor and are heavy laden, and I will give you rest. Take my yoke upon you, and learn of me; for I am meek and lowly in heart: and ye shall find rest unto your souls. For my yoke is easy, and my burden is light.

In planning the conference I prayed for the men who would preach Jesus to us. As the time of the conference drew near, I found myself praying often for all the pastors and their families who would listen to the messages. Perhaps much to the surprise of some, pastors are people. We, too, run the race right alongside the person in the pew. Like anyone else we may experience disillusionment, discouragement, heartache, and heartbreak. There is but one answer to any dilemma we may face . . . we must keep our eyes fixed upon Jesus looking not to the right nor to the left. We must have eyes only for Jesus. For those who needed comfort, I prayed for comfort. For those who needed conviction, I prayed for conviction. For those who needed cleansing, I prayed for cleansing. For those who needed courage, I prayed for courage.

Following the final sermon of the conference, I invited the entire assembly to kneel on the hard concrete floor of the Georgia World Congress Center and pray. As God's men and women knelt to pray I felt God's presence and rejoiced that "times of refreshing shall come from the presence of the Lord" (Acts 3:19). I saw tears of release and relief and I thanked God that seemingly His purpose had been served during the days we had joined together. We had come for the purpose of "looking unto Jesus," that we might go out and let others see Jesus in us. A world is waiting while there is a race to be run.

As you read these sermons may your heart be encouraged to run the race with renewed energy and enthusiasm for Jesus . . . Author and Finisher.

Morris H. Chapman
Pastor's Study
First Baptist Church
Wichita Falls, Texas

1
Run for the Finisher
By Morris Chapman

Morris H. Chapman

Morris H. Chapman has been pastor of the historic seventy-seven-hundred-member First Baptist Church, Wichita Falls, Texas, since February, 1979. He served as president of the Southern Baptist Convention's Pastors' Conference (1986) and is a member of the Board of Trustees of Hardin-Simmons University, Abilene, Texas. He served as chairman of the Committee on Order of Business of the Southern Baptist Convention (Dallas, 1985). He is the author of *Youth Affirm: The Doctrine of Christ* (Convention Press). He preaches on radio and television weekly. In 1980 the Freedom Foundation honored him for his sermon, "Hear This Word, America." He is a native of Kosciusko, Mississippi, and a graduate of Mississippi College (B.M.), Southwestern Baptist Theological Seminary (M.Div., D.Min.). He received the S.T.D. from Southwest Baptist University in 1985. He is married to the former Jodi Francis of Memphis, Tennessee. She is a trustee of the Sunday School Board of the Southern Baptist Convention and a member of the SBC Peace Committee. They have two children, Christopher and Stephanie.

1
Run for the Finisher

by Morris Chapman

Wherefore, seeing we also are compassed about with so great a cloud of witnesses, let us lay aside every weight, and the sin which doth so easily beset us, and let us run with patience the race that is set before us, Looking unto Jesus the author and finisher of our faith; who for the joy that was set before him endured the cross, despising the shame, and is set down at the right hand of the throne of God (Heb. 12:1-2).

The writer of Hebrews was saying there is a race to be run. He was writing against a backdrop of the Greek and Roman games. They had the Olypmic games at Mount Olympus, the Pythian games at Delphi, and the Isthmian games at Corinth. For men to run well in the races of that day, they had to train rigorously for months. A man had to discipline himself. He had to deny himself certain earthly pleasures. He would run under the hot summer sun. He would run against the howling winter winds. He would run, he would run, he would run. He would run until his heart beat with the cadence, "You are born to run. You are born to run."

The Word of God says that Christians are to run, to train

rigorously until our very hearts beat with that same cadence: "You are born to run. You are born to run." While we are in training our hearts will pound within us, "You are born to preach. You are born to preach."

My own memory has reverberated through the years with the prayer my mother prayed before I was born. For five years she was married without bearing a child and she prayed, "Lord, give me a child and I'll give him back to You." With great wisdom and understanding my mother said nothing about that prayer while I was growing up. At age seven I came to know the Lord Jesus Christ as my Savior. At age twelve I gave my life into God's Kingdom's service and, finally, at age sixteen, my mother told me about her prayer.

But God had already set the course. God had already sounded the call. I remember the Friday night at a Royal Ambassador camp in central Mississippi when I wanted more than anything in the world to do the Will of God. I wanted to do the Will of God so much I thought my heart would burst and as a twelve-year-old boy I walked down the aisle during the invitation. I came to the front of the room and there was a counselor who led me into the inquiry room. There he began to inquire, "What is your name? What is your address? What is the name of your church?" And then he said, "Son, what is your decision?" I answered, "I believe God is calling me into special service." He replied, "Well, I have some boxes here to check so that we will know what specialized area it is into which God is calling you." He asked, "Is God calling you to be a preacher?" Well, I was old enough to recognize that preachers only work one day a week and yet the idea of preaching was terrifying to me and I said, "No sir, God is not calling me to be a preacher."

He said, "Well, Son, is God calling you to be a minister of

education?" I said, "No sir. If I ever finish high school I'm finished with education." He replied, "Well, Son, I have another box. Is God calling you to be a minister of music?" And I said, "No sir, there seems to be so little music in my bones." By this time he was getting a little exasperated and he asked, "Well, Son, is God calling you to be a missionary?" The answer was easy. Africa was the only mission field I knew about and I just didn't think I had the courage to face up to the jungles of Africa so I said, "No, sir, God is not calling me to be a missionary." Providentially, since that time I have preached in Africa and would have been thrilled had God called me to be a missionary to that great continent.

In utter dismay he looked at me. He looked at the card. He looked at me again and he said, "Son, I've just got one more box." I said, "What is it?" He answered, "Other." I said, "Check it." And that night I gave my life to being "Other" for the Lord Jesus Christ.

We are running a race and we have been born into a family of runners. A part of the family has already gone before us. In verse 1 it says, "We are compassed about with so great a cloud of witnesses." These who watch us run the race are those who already have run the race. They have gone before us. They are now with God cheering us on. You say, "Who are these who have gone on before us?" Well, they are those who have lived by faith and died in the Lord. They are represented in the names of the heroes mentioned in Hebrews 11.

You will remember by reading through Hebrews 11 that the great saints and prophets are mentioned. They are the heroes of Hebrews and I want you to see where their faith led them. Beginning in chapter 11, verse 33, we are told how these men ran by faith. Now what do we do by faith? What is the opportunity of faith? In verse 33, the Bible says, "Who through faith." Now hear this: what they did, they did by faith. What did they do by faith? They subdued kingdoms. They wrought righteousness. They obtained promises. They stopped the mouths of lions. They quenched the violence of fire. They escaped the edge of the sword. Out of the weakness, they were made strong. They turned to flight the armies of the aliens. The women received their dead raised to life again. Others were tortured, not accepting deliverance that they might obtain a better resurrection. Still others had trials of cruel mockings and scourgings, bonds and imprisonment.

They were stoned. They were sawn asunder. They were tempted. They were slain with the sword. They wandered about in sheepskins and goatskins, being destitute and afflicted. They were tormented. They wandered in deserts, in mountains, and in dens and caves of the earth. And these heroes of Hebrews, these heroes of faith, having obtained a good report through faith, did not even receive the promise (see Hebrews 11:33-39). That simply means that they had not experienced the promise of the coming Messiah. They were heroes of faith although they had not seen Jesus. They were heroes of faith although Jesus had yet to come to earth to die on the cross. They were heroes of faith although Jesus had not yet been resurrected from the grave. They staked their all on a promise which God would not fulfill in their lifetimes.

But now Jesus had come! In Mark 2:1 we read that as Jesus walked into the city of Capernaum, the crowds whispered throughout the city, "Jesus has come! Jesus has come!" The Bible tells us in verse 2 that the crowds were so great there was hardly room to receive them and Jesus "preached the word unto them." Jesus *has* come! We must herald the Word to the world!

During my first pastorate in Rogers, Texas, a gentle, red-faced giant man of German descent said to me, "Preacher, do you know why my cows come when I call? They come because they know they'll be fed." We are to feed the world the Word of God. The word was out, "Jesus has come." Then Jesus preached the word unto them. We are to preach that "Jesus has come." We are to invite the unsaved to come to Jesus! The invitation to the world is in the words of the hymn, "Softly and Tenderly."

> Come home . . . come home
> Ye who are weary come home;
> Earnestly, tenderly, Jesus is calling,
> Calling, O sinner, come home!

The promise of God to the prophets of old has been fulfilled. My soul cries out within me, "Lord, but what have I done for Thee? Where is my conviction? Where is my courage? What price have I paid in serving the One who gave His all for me?"

What shall we do? Jesus saw the multitude of Jerusalem and He wept over them. His heart was burdened at their hardheartedness and yet everyday we see those who are being lost into an eternal hell without Jesus Christ die by the teeming thousands and millions. We see them lost. We look at them. Do we weep over them? Are our hearts burdened about them? We analyze them, we catagorize them, we talk about evangelizing them, but we rarely agonize over them. I tell you there will be no spiritual awakening among us until we are broken before God. When we are broken before God, we will become bold before men. The power of God will fall and the fires of revival will be ignited.

Our prayer ought to be, "Oh, dear Lord, teach us how to run the race." The writer of Hebrews gave us an instruction manual. He listed three elements of the race in verses 1 and 2:

preparation for the race; performance in the race; and preoccupation with the race.

Notice in verse 1 the preparation for the race. He said, "Let us lay aside every weight, and the sin which doth so easily beset us." First of all he said, "Let us lay aside every weight." That word *weight* literally means "encumbrance." So the Bible says we ought to lay aside every encumbrance in running our race for God. Now the runner likes to run with the wind. The runner strips down to nearly nothing because when he runs he wants to be light. He wants nothing to slow him down. You see, the word *weight* means any encumbrance which will slow him down in the race. An encumbrance is a thing that may not be necessarily wrong in itself but nevertheless it is wrong for us because we are running the race.

You see, anything that slows you down in reaching the goal that God has for you is encumbrance. Anything that keeps you from reaching the goal is wrong for you. And so the writer said, "Whatever the encumbrance, lay it aside."

Now you may be the only one who knows the encumbrance with which you are running the race. You may be the only one who can recognize it. Nobody knows it but you. There is little purpose in your pilgrimage, there is little power in your preaching, and the devil has you exactly where he wants you. Do you know why? Because you are running a half-hearted race. You began with a spring, but now you are finishing with a stagger. You once had boundless energy, now you are running with boring fatigue. You are just simply weighted down. Perhaps you have determined that your next step is going to lead you to the sideline. You are going to give it up. The load is too heavy. It is too much to bear and yet the words of Jesus are, "Come unto me all ye that labor and are heavy laden, and I will give you rest. Take my yoke upon you and learn of me . . .

for my yoke is easy and my burden is light" (Matt. 11:28-30).

If there is an encumbrance that has dragged you down and almost driven you out of the race, if you will lay it aside, Jesus will pick it up. He'll carry the burden for you. God has set you into a family of runners. He wants you to run that race with all the spiritual energy you can muster by the flowing power from the Holy Spirit of God. Lay aside the encumbrance—anything that slows you down, even if you don't think it's sin but you know it's slowing you down. You know it has diverted your energy from the things of God. You know you have put too much thought into it. Whatever it is, lay it aside.

Now in running the race, God says not only to lay aside every encumbrance, He also instructs us to remove every entanglement. He said, "Lay aside the sin which so easily beset you." Now that sin is what we might call an entanglement. Lay aside not only the encumbrance, the thing that slows you down. Also lay aside every entanglement. Whatever it is that will trip you up, lay it aside. The phrase "easily beset" means anything that would entangle us, anything that would wrap itself around us, anything that would trip us up. Do you know what the writer of Hebrews was saying? "Don't try to run the race which God has set before you with your tennis shoes tied together." That's it. Don't run with something that will trip you up. Don't run with an entanglement. Don't run with sin in your life because it will trip you up.

You may be struggling. In spite of all you try to do, you may find yourself at a point of friendship with sin. You try not to think about it but deep in your heart you know that sooner or later it is going to trip you up. You know when it does it is going to cost you dearly. Is there any sin in your life which you cherish? God's says, "Lay it aside. Lay it aside before it does trip you up."

The Bible says King David was a great man. He was "a man after God's own heart" (1 Sam. 13:14). Yet David lusted after Bathsheba. He committed adultery. He tried to cover by deceiving Bathsheba's husband. He made him drunk and later had him killed. Then he tried to carry on his royal duties in the usual way. But you see, sin is like a physical disease. The germ first invades the body. Infection sets in. There is a gradual decline. The disease breaks out. We lose our spiritual appetite and before we know it there is a collapse on the track of life.

Sin is alluring and attractive for the moment, but sin nearly killed David. He declared, "Day and night thy hand was heavy upon me" (Ps. 32:4). "My sin is ever before me" (Ps. 51:3). David sinned and it cost him his health (see Ps. 32:3-4). David sinned and it cost him his joy (see Ps. 51). David sinned and it cost him his family. David sinned and it almost cost him his kingdom. For you see, the Bible says, "When lust hath conceived it bringeth forth sin: when it is finished, it bringeth forth death" (Jas. 1:15). You see, sin is deceitful and subtle. You may not sense it at first until all of a sudden you find yourself ensnared with sin. Sin dims the eye until spiritual vision is clouded. Sin deafens the ear until God's voice is muted. Sin dulls the taste until you no longer hunger and thirst after righteousness.

The Bible says, "Love not the world . . . for all that is in the world, the lust of the flesh, and the lust of the eyes, and the pride of life, is not of the Father, but is of the world" (1 John 2:15-16). David cried out to God for help! He said,

Wash me thoroughly from mine iniquity, and cleanse me from my sin . . . Create in me a clean heart, O God; and renew a right spirit within me . . . Restore unto me the joy of thy salvation and uphold me with thy free spirit (Ps. 51:2,10,12).

David desperately wanted once again to "hear joy and gladness" (Ps. 51:8). That's the way it is when you get into sin. You say, "Oh, if I could just have the joy I once had. If I just had the purity I once had. If I just had the power I once had. If I just had the gladness I once had." If we are not careful we will become entangled in this world's pleasures, possessions, and popularity. And though we love Jesus, we will lose our joy. If you live for salary, you will lose your joy. If you live for self, you will lose your joy. If you live for sin, you'll lose your joy. But if you live for the Savior, you'll find an everlasting joy. Why? Because "in thy presence is fulness of joy" (Ps. 16:11).

When David confessed his sin, he began to walk in the joy of the Lord. Do you want to walk in joy? Do you want to walk in peace? Do you want to walk in power? Do you want to walk in the path of answered prayer? Then confess your sin. Confess those things that entangle you and trip you up. Confess those things that encumber you and load you down. Pray, "Lord, I don't want to be slowed down in the race. Forgive me. Turn me loose. Set me free."

Some years ago there was a man who lived in England named Billy Bray. Billy Bray was brash, loud, and boisterous. One day he got saved, and when Billy Bray got saved, he had no inhibitions whatsoever. He loved God so much that he shared the Lord everywhere he went. People began to ridicule him, laugh at him, and say, "Why Billy Bray, you are so happy and joyous all the time but what if you die and you find out you're not saved and you go to hell?" Billy Bray said, "Well, I'll tell you this. Suppose I do die and go to hell. Jesus has been so real, so wonderful, and so precious to me in this life that I will shout all the way to hell. When I get down to hell, I'll run up and down the streets of hell shouting, 'Hallelujah, praise the Lord!' The devil will come over to me and say, 'Billy Bray, we cannot stand for that down here. We're going to have to send you to heaven.'"

To have joy in running the race, God-appointed, God-anointed preachers must lay aside every encumbrance and every entanglement.

The writer of Hebrews told about the preparation for the race. Then he spoke of the performance in the race. He wrote, "And let us run with patience the race that is set before us" (Heb. 12:1). The word *race* literally means an athletic contest. The Greek word *agon* is where we get the English word *agony*. An athletic contest is a contest of agony. It takes all the energy within us. The race we are running is not without agony. Sometimes there is conflict in marriage. Sometimes there is conflict in ministry. God knows the race is not always easy. He says, "Run the race with patience" and the word *patience* is the word which means "to run with endurance." We are to remain under the pressure.

That's not the game people are playing in America today. They run from everything. They try to escape. If they don't like their job, they run from their job. If they don't like their spouse, they run from their spouse. Don't lose sight of the source of the pressure. Sometimes we become so engrossed in battling buildings and budgets that we forget we are at war against principalities, powers, rulers of darkness of this world, spiritual wickedness in high places (see Eph. 6:12). That's the opposition and no matter the opposition, God forbid that we ever lose heart, that we ever fail to endure under the pressure, that we ever let our voices be silenced. We are to be prophets of God and not puppets of the world. We are to be ruled by conviction and not by convenience. We are to long for the praise of God and not for human praise. Let it be recorded that we shall stand in the gap and speak a word for Jesus until He comes or until He calls us home. If we don't do it, who will?

The author of Hebrews wrote about preparation for the race. "Lay aside every encumbrance. Lay aside every entanglement." He wrote of the performance in the race. He said, "Run, remaining under the pressure. Endure to the end even though sometimes you would like to quit. And he told about the preoccupation of the race in Hebrews, chapter 12, verse 2. He said that we are to run the race "looking unto Jesus." Our race is going to end in a photo-finish . . . *looking* unto Jesus. The Greek word for *looking* means "to turn your eyes away from other things and fix them upon one thing."

I heard of a young woman who grew up in a wealthy home. One day she became a Christian. She was scolded by her father and ridiculed by her mother. Her father told her to renounce her newfound faith or forfeit her family inheritance. He gave her several days to think it over.

When the morning came, she sat down at the piano and her answer was in the song she played and sang.

> Jesus, I my cross have taken,
> All to leave and follow Thee;
> Destitute, despised, forsaken,
> Thou, from hence, my all shalt be;
> Perish every fond ambition,
> All I've sought and hoped and known;
> Yet how rich is my condition,
> God and heaven are still my own!

Jesus is the Author. He is our Example. Keep your eyes on Him. We get in our worst trouble when our eyes drift from Jesus and turn to the things of the world. He is our Example.

We can run because Jesus has run. We can endure because Jesus has endured. We can finish because Jesus has finished. He is our Finisher. That is, He is also our Enabler. He is the One who enables us. He is the One who empowers us.

Paul said to Timothy, "Stir up the gift of God, which is in thee . . . for God hath not given us the spirit of fear; but of power and of love, and of a sound mind" (2 Tim. 1:6-7). The gun has sounded. The race has begun. It is time to run. We are in a race which already has been won! When we know the Victor, we can claim the victory. If God has anointed you to preach, never give up, never give in, and you'll never give out.

The Bible says, "There is a way that seemeth right unto a man but the end thereof are the ways of death" (Proverbs 14:12). The world runs for a corruptible crown but we are running for an incorruptible crown (see 1 Cor. 9:24–25). For me that crown need be nothing more than a word from Jesus, "Well done, thou good and faithful servant" (Matt. 25:21).

The unsaved have nothing but a finish, but the saved have a Finisher. Look unto Jesus. Run for the Finisher. Our occupation is preaching. Our preoccupation is Jesus. God has called us not to magnify ourselves, but to glorify Him. "God forbid that I should glory, save in the cross of our Lord Jesus Christ" (Gal. 6:14). Run for the Finisher!

2
Who Jesus Is

By Harold Carter

Harold A. Carter

Harold A. Carter, a native of Selma, Alabama, has been pastor of New Shiloh Baptist Church, Baltimore, Maryland, for twenty-two years. Formerly he was pastor of Court Street Baptist Church, Lynchburg, Virginia. His education includes Ph.D. degrees from St. Mary's Ecumenical University, Baltimore, Maryland, and Colgate Bexler Hall/Crozer Seminary, Rochester, New York. He has authored eight books. His first book was *The Prayer Tradition of Black People* (1976). His family includes his wife, Weptanomah W. Carter, author of *The Black Minister's Wife,* and two children, Harold A. Carter, Jr., and Weptanomah B. Carter.

2
Who Jesus Is

by Harold Carter

I praise God for your theme, "Jesus: Author and Finisher." I have been assigned the topic "Who Jesus Is." Quite honestly, it's the sweetest topic I think any fundamental, Bible-believing, Holy Ghost-filled preacher might wish to preach.

Walking home from church this morning, I met some of the pastors from Texas and one asked me, "Brother, what are you going to preach tonight?" I said, "Who Jesus Is." Then I said, "You know, that subject has no middle ground. Either you make it or you flunk. You don't play the fence on this one. He is either your Savior or He is your Judge."

I'm happy tonight to tell you that He is the Savior and Lord of my life. He has lifted me out of the pits. He has given purpose to my life and I call Him my Lord. He inspires me to preach His Word, He gives me courage to live a victorious life and in Him I live, move, and have my eternal being. Like Jeremiah, He is like fire shut up in my bones and I love Him so much that I have a burning desire that all persons who occupy a space on planet earth might also know even as I know that Jesus is the Light of the world.

I have chosen as a basis of my message the first four verses of Titus 1.

> Paul, a servant of God, and an apostle of Jesus Christ, according to the faith of God's elect, and the acknowledging of the truth which is after godliness; In hope of eternal life, which God, that cannot lie, promised before the world began; But hath in due times manifested his word through preaching, which is committed unto me according to the commandment of God our Saviour; to Titus, mine own son after the common faith: Grace, mercy, and peace, from God the Father and the Lord Jesus Christ our Saviour.

Paul did not always talk like this. In fact, being a Jew from Tarsus, a Pharisee by religious party, eloquent of mind and spirit, he rose to the top of his generation and went out to destroy the church. To him Jesus was a fraud and an insurrectionist, a misguided Jew who had to be put out. But en route to Damascus, Syria, the Lord Jesus Christ met him in a vision. The One Paul thought was an insurrectionist suddenly became his Lord. And it was out of this context that the apostle Paul forever made as the declaration of his life the statement that we find in Philippians 3,

> I want to know Jesus and I want to be impacted by the power that flows from His resurrection. I want to share in the fellowship of His suffering and I want my life to be made conformable to His glorious and resurrected image. I want to know Jesus (author's paraphrase).

Thus in this salutation to Titus, Paul not only told us about his great devotion to the Lord, but he laid down four major pillars that give a biblically complete foundation to an insight on who Jesus really is.

First of all Paul said, "I am a servant." And that's a key word because no man or woman can really know the Lord until you become His servant. You must remember that you were sold to the bondage of sin, that you were cast into the quicksand of deprivation, you were on your way to hell without excuse, and yet out of God's great mercy, He sent His servant whose name is Jesus. He released our captivity. He broke our bond. He announced the year of jubilee. Because of His perfect Sonship to God, Jesus, through faith in Him, made it possible for us to become sons and daughters of the Most High God.

Therefore we are servants. We must hear what He says, go where He tells us, do what He said do. We must obey Him, not persons. We are servants of God and once you become a servant of God, you can say with Paul, "All that I am and all that I hope to be, I owe it to the Lord." Not only say, "I'm a servant," which is a qualification of getting to know Jesus, he said, "I am an apostle, one who has seen the Lord, one who is a student of the Lord, one whose devotion is to know Him. I am an apostle."

And I make bold to declare that every born-again, blood-washed servant of God can still see Jesus. 1 John 5 tells us there are three that agree on earth: The water, the blood and the Spirit. We need the waters for holy baptism to wash away sin and to indicate a change of life that comes over us once we are transformed by His grace. We need the blood to generate us so that we are not worshipping in human power—flesh power— but under the anointing of the Holy Spirit. And we need the Spirit to give us a real authority over the things of the world.

Therefore, I have come to say tonight what the Beatitudes said, "Blessed are the pure in heart for they shall see God" Matt. 5:8. It was out of this context that Paul, writing to a Gentile Christian, which was revolutionary in and of itself for the gospel, had already moved over to a Gentile and said to him, "Titus, I want you to carry forth the work but I want you to carry forth recognizing what I've already said, that you are to do it knowing always who Jesus is." Who is Jesus? Paul first of all said to Titus that Jesus is the Word of Promise. Here is what he said: God cannot lie. God promised a Redeemer, not to humanity, but to Himself. We have no good works which command God to do anything. Naked came we into this world and naked we are going to leave here. We have no righteousness, but God promised Jesus for His own Namesake.

The Bible declares that the Lord God Almighty, being omniscient, knows human problems even before we fall into them. The other day in Russia a nuclear explosion almost destroyed thousands of people and only God knows how many will come down with cancer or whatever. Russian scientists had to rush in after the fact because people react but God does not have to react. God knows tomorrow's headlines yesterday. God has an ambulance waiting on life's roadway before the accident happens.

Hebrews 10:7 says, "Lo, I come." In the book of Jude we read in the 14th verse, "And Enoch also, the seventh from Adam, prophesied of these, saying, Behold, the Lord cometh with ten thousands of his saints." He is going to bring judgment on the sons and daughters of men. I tell you, this gospel we preach is not some invention of some theologian, it's not something cooked up in some library by some Dr. This or Professor That. This Word of God has been promised. Therefore I don't need to get mixed up under the impact of some new-day cult, some new-day "ism."

Almost every week I get a letter inviting me on a free trip to Korea. I don't need to go to Korea to know what the promise is. I know what the promise is. There are always persons with some other promise. We read about the cults in news magazines and other publications. Too often we see the adherents of these cults at airports, streets, and of all things even in a school system that does not want Jesus. Many of them even get in the schools. But I have come to tell you, I'm neither rocking to nor fro by the winds of these cults.

I hear the apostle Paul telling every Timothy and every Titus, "You don't have to go here and yonder looking for the promise, you stand on the Word of God and you are on the Promise." For God's Word, not human words, but God's Word will never fail. God cannot lie. Man will lie and does lie but what God says, you can sleep on. You can get up on it. Whatever may happen, you can believe He is saying, "Lo, I'll be with you always."

He's not only the Word of Promise, but this Jesus is the Word of Proclamation. For He declared in His Word that in due times He was manifested through the word of preaching. The devil has tried to get a lot of us to feel you can shift the emphasis from the pulpit to activity. Boy Scouts are good. Tea suppers are alright. Social activities have their place. But the only way God has provided that lost sinners may be saved and that people on their way to hell might be turned around is through the preaching of the Word of God. Thank God for good choirs. I love this choir. I love the orchestration but I've never read anywhere in the Word of God that singing can save anybody. It will help to drive the devil out. It will help to get you on one accord. It will help to make long-faced people smile. It will help to loosen you up but the only way you are going to realize that "I'm a sinner, I am devil bound and on my way to hell," is to realize you need the grace of God to lift you up and turn you around.

The God-fearing, Holy Ghost-filled man of God must stand up and declare the unsearchable riches of God. He must do it under the anointing of God's power by preaching. I hear all this stuff about sermonettes and I don't know what a sermonette is and if you've got any sermonettes, you ought to go home tonight and throw every one of them away. There are people in church now who don't preach more than fifteen minutes and if you get beyond twenty minutes you have violated every law. Well, some sermons are not even fit to go twenty minutes because if the Lord's not in it, it's no good anyhow.

On the other hand, if the Lord is moving and the Holy Ghost is moving from heart to heart and soul to soul and the people have their eyes on Jesus, I don't care how long the man preaches. I don't care how long he is under the anointing. I tell you, you can't get enough of the Word of God. Tell me the story of Jesus. "I love to tell the story. It will be my theme in glory. To tell the old, old story of Jesus and His love."

I thank God for the Southern Baptist Convention. I've been blessed to preach at many of our state meetings and in a national meeting. Always in these settings I remember how seed planted on the water still bears fruit. At one time the Southern Baptist Convention years and years ago underwrote my own father's teaching at a Baptist school in Selma, Alabama. My Daddy, soon to be eighty-four, is still pastoring two churches in Alabama. He doesn't know anything about the new doctrine of retiring. Down in Alabama they believe they are faithful unto death, "And I will give thee a crown of life" (Rev. 2:10).

The older I get the more I'm beginning to think that also. Because as I look at my father and think of how he has been preaching this gospel, I think about here I am preaching this same old gospel. I've seen what the Lord can do, I've seen what this gospel anointed at Pentecost can do and now I look at myself preaching the same gospel, pastoring a church.

When you preach the gospel of proclamation, it brings everybody together in one accord. I don't care whether you are Oriental, Hispanic, blonde, brunette, thick-lipped, or thin-lipped, every man or woman needs the Word of God. I want to tell you when this gospel is preached, I don't care who is sitting next to you, you forget about who is next to you and begin to say, "Thank You, Lord. Thank You for dying for my sin."

Not only will this gospel bring everybody to one accord, but this gospel gives us one message. Nobody had to write me about my theology because I believe the Bible. I didn't sign any covenant to come here. I believe the Book and I tell you, if you believe the Book, you won't get mixed up anywhere. People in Korea need the Book. People in Cuba need the Book. I don't care where you go, everybody wants to know about Jesus for He is the One who makes it all possible.

When I was over in the Philippines, incidentally sent by Southern Baptists for about five or six weeks, I got over there in those bamboo churches and I was preaching through an interpreter and I was getting one complaint night after night. What was the complaint? They said, "It's too short." Now I'm preaching an hour and a half and they say I'm too short. I tried to get it up to two hours and I was worn out but they were still saying it was too short. They had no air conditioning, they had nothing like we've got here. All they wanted to do was hear about Jesus.

I'm afraid today that we don't want to hear about Jesus because we had rather have culture than Christ. Culture can't save you. Soft pews and pretty buildings won't save you. Hallelujah! The only One who can wash away your sin is Jesus.

I've come tonight to tell you brothers and sister, I'm not going to let culture rob me of my joy. I love the Lord tonight. Oh, I thank God for the education I have but it's not going to rob me of Jesus. I thank God for the blessings I have but it's not going to rob me of Jesus. I want to encourage every preacher out there, go back to your community, your churches, your evangelistic stations, hold up this precious Book and preach it under the authority of Almighty God. If you've been scared to sweat, sweat a little bit. If you've been scared to lift up your voice, lift it up anyhow. Let the world know you are going to do what the Lord said do. "Lift up thy voice like a trumpet and show my people their transgression (Isa. 58:1).

Here in Titus 1 the apostle Paul said not only word of proclamation but oh, I'm glad to say, here is the word of *participation* which God has given us. He said, "In the common faith. In the common faith." Thank God for Martin Luther who recognized nearly five-hundred years ago that the priests didn't know it all. No, no, no. Martin Luther read the Word, that the "just must live by faith" (Hak. 2:4).

They've got dugouts in baseball. God does not have any dugouts in the church. Everybody gets on the field and plays. They've got sidelines in football but God does not have any sideline benches. You may not sing like the angels but you can do something. You may not preach like the preacher but you can say *Amen*. You may not sing like this choir, but the Lord wants everybody to participate. I want to tell you that wherever the Word of God is preached people will inevitably say, "What must I do?" Maybe we are not preaching hard enough. What must I do?

I had to smile and laugh in the hotel this afternoon. My wife was listening to a preacher on the radio and he was just preaching his head off. Suddenly he said, "I'm talking to you. Why don't you talk to me?" She started smiling. She said, "I haven't heard that one." I want to tell you, when the preacher talks to you, you've got to go out and talk to the world.

Oh, how we need members in the Body of Christ to go out and tell the abortionists that life is sacred, that the human body is the temple of the Almighty God. Hallelujah! Oh, how we need to go out and tell these corrupted people that pornography is about to destroy civilization. And you can make up your bed in sexual immorality but I tell you, if you sow to the wind, you are going to reap the whirlwind. Oh, how we need to tell this narcissistic, pleasure-oriented generation that pleasure will take you to hell.

Oh, how we need to tell this mixed-up generation that loves to lotterize itself, that loves Atlantic City and Las Vegas, that God is the only real "Hit" you need. Not the things of the world but Jesus is the only One you need and the only way you are going to do it. Preacher, you can't do it by yourself. You need somebody to pray with you. You need somebody to hold up the hand of Jesus with you. "And I, if I be lifted up from the earth, will draw all men unto me" (John 12:32). And I believe during this week we've come because everyone of us wants to go back and participate a little bit more. Why? This Jesus is not only the Word of Promise, He is not only the Word of Proclamation, He is not only the Word of Participation, He is the Word of Perfection.

I don't care what anybody says, Jesus said, "Be ye therefore perfect, even as your heavenly Father is perfect" (Matt. 5:48). I want to tell you, you can't do it by yourself. That's why the Lord said, "When I'm gone, I'm going to send the Holy Ghost." Now there was a time Baptists used to believe in and love the Holy Ghost. I'm not saying we don't believe in the Holy Ghost anymore, but I want to remind you that literature may help you, but you still need some power. Ecclesiastical organization will help you, but you still need power. There's only one way you are going to have power. You've got to have the Holy Spirit. For when you have the Holy Spirit, in the twinkling of an eye, He can do for you what you can't do for yourself.

I saw the Lord up there on Mount Calvary and there were two thieves, one on the left, one on the right. The one on the left became fatalistic. "If you are the Son of God, why don't you save us?" The one on the right said, "Why don't you shut up?" The first thief was like many today who think religion is a waste of time, who believe that preachers are just emotionalizers. There he was in the presence of the Lord. He could have had Perfection. He refused it. But the other brother said, "Lord, I've been listening to You. I heard You pray and deliver Your mother into Your disciples' hands. I heard You when you prayed for the whole world and said, 'Father, forgive them. They know not what they do.' Jesus, I know I'm not worthy, but when You come into Your kingdom, remember me."

I saw Jesus stop dying long enough to say, "Brother, I know you are on a cross, but today you shall be with Me in Paradise." The man did not come down and go to a New Member's Class; he did not come down and go through a discipleship class. In a moment, in the twinkling of an eye, Jesus washed him and made him holy in God's sight.

I want to tell you what the Lord can do for every one of us. In a few days the whole world is going to be looking at that place on Ellis Island called A Beautiful Lady. The lady is now 100 years of age. Along the way grime got on the lady. The lady's skin began to wrinkle. The nation looked around and found some French craftsmen who came over and combed her hair, fixed her face, powdered her lips, and got her looking real good. And on the Fourth of July of 1986, President Reagan will rededicate the lady who has welcomed people from all over the world. Political people, diplomats, people who have been kicked out of their country, black people, white people, Hispanics, everybody. I want to tell you, however high the lady is, there is a statue, not just a statue, there is a living Statute higher than the statue on Ellis Island. There is a Statue over there in a place called Jerusalem. That Statue has been there for almost two thousand years. It needs nobody to brush it up, it needs nobody to polish it up, it needs nobody to sign it up. That Statute was the same yesterday. That Statue is the same today and it will be tomorrow.

The Statue of Liberty may have welcomed just a handful but that other Statue says, "Whosoever will, let him come."

I want to close by saying I heard the voice of Jesus saying, "Come unto me and rest. Lay down thy weary soul. Lay down thy head upon my breast." I close by telling you I came to Jesus as I was. I was weary, wounded, and sad but I found in Him a resting place. He has made me glad. Oh praise God, when I leave this building, I will leave with that same benediction echoing in my heart, "And now unto him who is able" (see Jude 24). We are not able but Jesus is able to keep you from stumbling and falling. He is able to present you faultless before the throne of God with exceeding great joy.

To the only wise God, our Savior, be glory, honor, dominion and power. How long? Forever and ever. And when we've gone the last mile of the way and this old world can afford us a home no longer, when we are through preaching down here, when we can no longer sing down here, when we can no longer shed tears of joy down here, Oh God, when the saints go marching in, I want to be in that number to crown the King of King and Lord of Lords. Let's everybody say Amen!

3
Jesus: First and Forever

By Edwin Young

H. Edwin Young

H. Edwin Young, a native of Laurel, Mississippi, is pastor of Second Baptist Church, Houston, Texas. He was formerly pastor of the First Baptist churches of Columbia, South Carolina, Taylors, South Carolina, Canton, North Carolina, and Erwin, North Carolina. He has served on the General Board Executive Committee, South Carolina Baptist Convention, as a trustee of Southeastern Baptist Theological Seminary, as a trustee of the Baptist Sunday School Board, and as a member of the SBC Peace Committee. He was educated in the public schools of Laurel, Mississippi; received the B.A. from Mississippi College, Clinton; the B.D. from Southeastern Baptist Theological Seminary, Wake Forest, North Carolina; and the D.D. from Furman University, Greenville, South Carolina. Young is married to the former Jo Beth Landrum, and they have three sons, Edwin Barry, Benjamin Blake, and Clifford Wesley.

3
Jesus: First and Forever

By Edwin Young

Charles Schultz, in his cartoons, once painted a little picture of Lucy and Linus in their home looking out a window at a thunderstorm. Lucy, in typical candidness, said, "I hope it doesn't rain and rain until the whole world is flooded." Linus came back with, "Don't worry. In Genesis 9:13-14 God promised Noah that He would never again send a flood that would cover the whole earth and He put the rainbow in the sky as a promise that this would be true."

Lucy sighed and said, "That sure makes me feel a whole lot better." Linus replied, "Sound doctrine has a way of doing that."

We are going to look at a doctrine, beginning with a study of Revelation Chapter 5, verses 5 and 6, which say,

And one of the elders saith unto me, weep not: behold, the Lion of the tribe of Juda, the Root of David, hath prevailed to open the book, and to loose the seven seals thereof. And I beheld, and, lo, in the midst of the throne and of the four beasts, and in the midst of the elders stood a Lamb as it had been slain, having seven horns and seven eyes, which are the seven Spirits of God sent forth into all the earth.

Now notice verses 9-13.

And they sung a new song, saying, Thou art worthy to take the book, and to open the seals thereof: for thou wast slain, and hast redeemed us to God by thy blood out of every kindred, and tongue, and people, and nation; And hast made us unto our God kings and priests: and we shall reign on the earth. And I beheld, and I heard the voice of many angels sound about the throne, and the beasts, and the elders: and the number of them was ten thousand times ten thousand, and thousands of thousands; Saying with a loud voice, Worthy is the Lamb that was slain to receive power, and riches, and wisdom, and strength, and honor, and glory, and blessing. And every creature which is in heaven, and on the earth, and under the earth, and such as are in the sea, and all that are in them, heard I saying, Blessing, and honor, and glory, and power, be unto him that sitteth upon the throne, and unto the Lamb for ever and ever.

In my opinion, the most overlooked doctrine by homileticians is the Doctrine of the Preexistence of Jesus Christ. Jesus Christ did not come into the world the way that you and I came into the world. He did not come into being at the moment of His conception or birth. He existed prior to time.

We know that Jesus Christ was there in pre-Creation and was a part and parcel of the Creation. We know that Christ is depicted in the Old Testament. We know Christ is expanded in the New Testament as we see all the Messianic prophecies fulfilled and then we see Jesus Christ in post-historic times in Revelation, ruling and reigning through eternity forever.

The prologue of John's gospel introduces us to the concept of the preexistence of Christ. It says, "In the beginning was the Word" (John 1:1). John was saying, "Before anything was, there was that Word, there was that preexistent Christ." And then he said, "And the Word was with God." That little preposition *with* tells us there is a relationship between Jesus and God. There was that interpersonal relationship. Then John said, "The Word was God." This tells us that Jesus was Deity as the Father or God is Deity.

Now we look at the concept of this tremendous truth and we recognize that it is unfolded in the Bible in a beautiful, beautiful way. If you want to have your belief in the infallible, inerrant Word of God further established, begin a study of a doctrine of unfolding, a progressive revelation of truth. We see this so beautifully in the doctrine of the Lamb. Prior to creation was the Lamb. In the early foregleams of the Old Testament we see the Lamb.

Now when we study this progressive revelation, we must understand that many times when the word, phrase, or insight first appears, you have no way to know that this is just the first note of a developing chord which will move into a chorus that will progress to a mighty symphony in the end.

Now the idea of progressive revelation does not mean that the Bible moves from error to truth but it does mean that God's Word moves from the dim light of the dawn to the brilliance of the noonday. So many times a doctrine which begins in obscurity will develop page after page and chapter after chapter until finally somewhere in the New Testament we see the consummation of this doctrinal statement.

The doctrine of the Lamb is the best illustration of this I know. It begins really in the Garden of Eden in the first chapters of Genesis. We know that Adam and Eve were expelled from the garden. We know that God had them to remove their fig leaves and He put on them a skin.

God Himself killed an animal and clothed them with skin as they went out of the garden so their sin would be covered. We see in Hebrews 9:22 that without the shedding of blood there is no remission of sin. In Genesis, chapter 4 we see the progression develop just a little bit more.

There the offerings were brought from Cain and Abel. Abel came with an offering of the firstlings of the flock. He was obedient to God. Blood was shed. The lamb was slaughtered and we know that he found forgiveness from the Lord. We read about Abel's faith in Hebrews 11. But we look at Cain and at first balance it is a mystery as to why God Almighty would not accept the offering of Cain. He brought the fruit of the ground. He had cultivated and nurtured the ground. He brought the offering to the Lord but God rejected that offering. Why? Because Cain wanted to show what he had done. It was an indication of his own independence, of working out his own salvation, of cutting a separate deal independent from God.

It was a thing of self-reliance, a thing of display. We know it was grown from the ground that had already been cursed and therefore the offering of Cain was rejected. Therefore he did not find the forgiveness of the Lord. But right in the beginning of Genesis 4, we see the necessity of the Lamb. And then we move to Genesis 22 and we see that beautiful figure of Abraham, commanded by God to take his son, Isaac, to Mount Moriah and to offer him as a sacrifice. Now we know that God did not intend for Abraham to kill his son. What was that all about? Simply this: Isaac had taken the place that God only can have in a human heart. Therefore when Abraham took Isaac to Mount Moriah, God was testing Abraham's relationship to the Lord to reestablish it.

Then we remember that profound, timeless question which we read in the twenty-second chapter of Genesis. It is a very, very important question. It is a question we are hearing asked over and over again in an indefinite number of ways in our own day. We know that as they went up the mountain Isaac looked at Abraham and said, "You have the fire. You have the knife. You have the wood." This is the question: "Where is the lamb?" Abraham gave a timeless answer, "God will provide for Himself the lamb." Then we see how Abraham's hand was stayed with the knife, Isaac was released, and they looked over in a thicket and there was the ram. God had provided the lamb and the sacrifice was ordered.

Then we move on the next picture. First we saw in Genesis 4 the necessity of the lamb. In Genesis 22 we saw clearly that God would provide the lamb. Then in Exodus 12 we find the Passover picture. We know that every Hebrew family was commanded by God to kill a lamb and put the blood on the doorpost of their home so the death angel would pass over and spare that family from losing their firstborn son.

The emphasis in the Passover is the shed blood. The blood must be shed for the death angel to pass over. Then we move on to Leviticus 16. There we see the High Priest on the Day of Atonement. The lamb would be killed and the High Priest would bring it into the tabernacle. He would bring it into the holy place and would carefully take the blood and sprinkle it on the Mercy Seat. The Mercy Seat was the place where God would meet mankind. There we see the blood was applied and the sin of the nation found the forgiveness of God through the blood of the lamb.

Then we move to Isaiah 53. In this prophetic word we are taken even farther and a new and profound truth is revealed. For the first time in Scripture we see that the Lamb is not an animal but is really a Person. That's a tremendous, giant step into progressive unfolding doctrine of the Lamb. The Lamb becomes a Person. "God hath laid upon him," said Isaiah, in verse 6. We find a very familiar verse: "All we like sheep have gone astray." We see that the Lamb gathers strays.

Now if we understood more about sheep it would have made us mad to realize that Isaiah said, "You and I, we are like sheep." Now if you think sheep are warm and cuddly and beautiful and gentle little things, you don't know anything about sheep. Sheep are stubborn and most of them have parasites. They carry all kinds of diseases and there is no animal that is cared for by man on this earth that demands more attention. There is no animal that is dumber and those who know better than I say the stench from a sheep will turn your stomach twenty feet away. They get lost all the time. They are brutal to one another and Isaiah said, "All we like sheep have gone astray."

But we know that the Lamb gathers sheep in the progressive unfolding. What kind of Lamb? Every Eastern shepherd would raise in his own home a little lamb. He would take that lamb and it would become a pet. He would put a bell around that lamb's neck and wherever he would go, that little lamb would walk beside him and that lamb was called the "bell-wether." You have heard the phrase, "the big fullback on our team and the middle linebacker, he's our 'bellwether.'" This means, "That's the one we can count on." We see this little sheep, this bellwether and when one of the sheep would wander off and get lost, the bellwether would go out and the lost sheep would hear the ringing of the bell and know the shepherd was close by. They would go find the sheep and bring that sheep back home.

Here is the picture, "All we like sheep have gone astray," and that Lamb goes out and gathers in strays. But look how it moves. Finally we know all the progressiveness here involved in the Lamb but we go on to the gospel of John. Not only is the Lamb a Person but the Lamb is further identified in John, chapter 1 by John the Baptist as he looked at Jesus and said, "Behold, the Lamb of God which taketh away the sin of the world."

The Lamb which we have seen in Genesis 4 has been progressively unfolding in the Scripture until now the Lamb is identified and it is this same Jesus. It says, "Behold, the lamb." Notice that, "*the* Lamb." Thousands of lambs had been slain in the tabernacle, in the temple. Millions of lambs had been slain. The qualification of the lamb would be without spot, without blemish and we know now *the* lamb was prepared . . . this Lamb without spot and without blemish is indeed Jesus Christ.

Now a spot would mean external problems—external sins. A blemish would be a blot or a stain within, like original sin. We know Jesus Christ was without external or internal sin. He was *the* lamb, a sacrifice that would take place on Calvary once and for all. He was the Lamb of God.

Mankind did not want to receive Jesus. The Bible says, "he came unto his own and his own received him not" John 1:11. But God sent the Lamb, for the Bible says, "Behold, the lamb of God which taketh away sin." In the Old Testament sin was covered by the blood and we see in this passage in the New Testament that sin was not only covered by the blood but the blood washed the sin away. That is, the blood took all the sin away. "That taketh away the sin,"—what?—"The sin of the world." The whole world. We go to 1 Peter and see that Peter told us this was a Lamb that was slain before the foundation of the world.

We see the progressive unfolding of the Lamb in Genesis. In chapter 2 we see that the Lamb was for sin. In Genesis 22 we see the Lamb was for that one person, Isaac. In Exodus 12 we see the Lamb was for the family that had the blood applied. In Leviticus 16 we see that the Lamb was there for the whole nation on the Mercy Seat. In John 1 we see that the Lamb was slain for the whole world. In 1 Peter we see that the Lamb was slain in the mind of God in the preexistent state before the foundation of the world, before its beginning.

But the Lord's not through yet. We go to Revelation 5 and that's the scripture which I read. While John was on Patmos he began to weep and he said, "Oh, who will open these seven seals?" We know that these seven seals represent the title deeds to the universe and none was worthy until finally through the inspired pen comes that word, "Oh yes, there is One that is worthy. There is One that is worthy. He is the Lion of Juda. He is the root of David." The Lion of Juda is a Messianic word and the root of David goes back and refers to the preexistence of this same Lamb, this same Jesus.

We see John looking on the throne and he said, "I am going to see the Lion of Juda." But he is shocked. He says, "Lo, woe, behold, on the throne is"—what?—In the Greek it says, "A little Lamb." A little Lamb is on the throne. There we see in all of glory that voices of praise are raised. Over and over again in the rest of the chapter, "Worthy is the Lamb. Worthy is the Lamb." The Lamb was in the tabernacle and the Light of heaven was the Lamb. The Lamb was in the throne and the throne was in the Book of Life. "Worthy, worthy is the Lamb."

But we're not through yet. Because we go to Revelation 21 and Revelation 22 and there we see a new heaven and a new earth. All the sin, greed, shame, suffering, death, tears, and sorrow have passed away. There on the throne in a New Jerusalem we see once again the Lamb. Now the victim has become the Victor. The crucified has become the Crown. The Servant has become the Savior. We see the Lamb ruling and reigning throughout all eternity forever and forever.

Nine significant passages. Look at them: the Lamb for sin; the Lamb for one person; the Lamb for one family; the Lamb for one nation; the Lamb for the elect; the Lamb for the world; the Lamb for all history; the Lamb for all the universe; and, finally, the Lamb for all eternity.

Here is a final brief word. You find a church that's dead, cold, stale, and lifeless and you'll find a church that shuns the preaching of the Lamb and the blood of Jesus Christ. You'll find a church that is practicing the religion of Cain. A bouquet of flowers and fruits they bring but there is no mention of the blood of the Lamb because of our scholarship, because of the intelligentsia, because of our erudition.

Now let me tell you something. My brethren, never be ashamed to proclaim the Lamb and the blood of Jesus Christ which covers and takes away sin because, when this happens, the church is always alive. Our calling is the same commission that John the Baptist had. It is simply to look up to Him as He has been lifted up and say to everybody all the time and every-day—just point to Him and say, "Behold the Lamb of God which taketh away the sin of the world."

4
The Cradle That Rocked the World

By Adrian Rogers

Adrian P. Rogers

Dr. Adrian P. Rogers has been pastor of the Bellevue Baptist Church, Memphis, Tennessee, since 1972. He has served two terms as president of the Southern Baptist Convention.

A native of West Palm Beach, FL, he is a graduate of Stetson University (B.A.) and New Orleans Baptist Theological Seminary (Th.M.). He has been awarded honorary doctorates from five educational institutions.

He has served his denomination in many capacities, including president of the Southern Baptist Convention's Pastors' Conference. At present he is a member of the SBC Peace Committee. He has been a trustee of Union University, Jackson, TN, and Luther Rice Seminary, Jacksonville, FL. In addition, he has been on the advisory council or board of reference for several other seminaries and institutions of higher learning.

Dr. Rogers is married to the former Joyce Gentry of West Palm Beach, FL. They have four grown children—Steve, Gayle, David, and Janice.

Under his leadership Bellevue has grown to over seventeen thousand members—and is still growing. Dr. Rogers's greatest joy centers in his relationship to Jesus Christ, his family, and the church he pastors.

He is the author of two books, *God's Way to Health, Wealth, and Wisdom* (Broadman) and *The Secret of Supernatural Living.* His preaching ministry is spread widely through radio, television, and tapes.

4

The Cradle That Rocked the World

by Adrian Rogers

In Luke, chapter 1, verses 26-35, the Bible says,

And in the sixth month the angel Gabriel was sent from God unto a city of Galilee, named Nazareth, To a virgin espoused to a man whose name was Joseph, of the house of David; and the virgin's name was Mary. And the angel came in unto her, and said, Hail, thou that art highly favored, the Lord is with thee: blessed art thou among women. And when she saw him, she was troubled at his saying, and cast in her mind what manner of salutation this should be. And the angel said unto her, Fear not, Mary: for thou hast found favor with God. And behold, thou shalt conceive in thy womb, and bring forth a son, and shalt call his name JESUS. He shall be great, and shall be called the Son of the Highest, and the Lord God shall give unto him the throne of his father David. And he shall reign over the house of Jacob for ever; and of his kingdom there shall be no end. Then said Mary unto the angel, How shall this be, seeing I know not a man? And the angel answered and said unto her, The Holy Ghost shall come upon thee, and the power of the Highest shall overshadow thee: therefore also that holy thing which shall be born of thee shall be called the Son of God.

Can you imagine that angel, Gabriel, dispatched from highest heaven, from the council halls of the Holy Trinity, with a message for a little maiden, Mary. He came to this sweet teenaged peasant girl and gave her the message that she was going to be the mother of the Messiah. And Mary said, "Behold, the hand maiden of the Lord; be it unto me according to thy word."

I see Gabriel as he ascended quick as a flash back to the highest heaven, gathered the other angels and the angelic choir, and said, "I have wonderful news, she has accepted. You've got nine months to rehearse." The angels' choirs began to rehearse and on that night they began to sing, "Glory to God in the highest and on earth, peace, good will to men."

I want you to see four basic thoughts about the virgin birth. Thought number one: the sinful mockery of His birth. Not everyone believes in the virgin birth of Jesus Christ. The late Harry Emerson Fosdick said, "I want to assure you that I do not believe in the virgin birth of Jesus Christ." Nels Ferré said this: "Jesus is the illegitimate child of a Roman soldier who had a love affair with Mary." Hugh Schoenfeld said this: "The virgin birth is a myth. The myth takes the reader out of this world of sober reality into the world of myth." And Bishop Robinson said this: "The virgin birth is a story on the level of an Andy Capp comic. It is true only in our imagination."

Over ten years ago, *Redbook* magazine surveyed Protestant seminaries, Protestant seminary students, and Protestant preachers and they found out that only 56 percent of the students in Protestant seminaries believed in the virgin birth of Jesus Christ.

If you do not accept the virgin birth of Jesus Christ as literal Bible truth, you've got some real problems. Number one: you have a problem with Mary and the character of Mary. If Jesus was not born of a virgin, Mary was a strumpet, a harlot, an impure woman. But not only do you have difficulty with the character of Mary, you have difficulty with the character of Jesus Christ. For if Jesus Christ was not the Son of God, Jesus Christ was the son of Adam and in Adam all die.

I'm going to tell you something else, dear friend, if Jesus Christ was not born of a virgin, you have difficulty with the character of this Book, for this Book says that "a virgin shall conceive and be with child." This Book says that Jesus was born of a virgin and if Jesus Christ is not virgin-born, you can have it, I don't want it because it is a bundle of blunders and a lie.

But I'm going to tell you something else. If you don't believe in the virgin birth of Jesus Christ, not only do you have difficulty with the character of Mary, the character of Jesus, and the character of the Word of God, but you've got a big difficulty in your own character. I wouldn't give you half a hallelujah for your chance of heaven if you don't believe in the virgin birth of Jesus Christ. You take the virgin birth out and the house of Christianity will collapse like a house of cards.

The second thing I want you to see, not only the sinful mockery of His birth, but the sacred mystery of His birth. "The angel said unto her, Fear not Mary, for thou hast found favor with God, And behold, thou shalt conceive in thy womb and bring forth a son and shalt call his name JESUS" (Luke 1:30-31). You say, "Adrian, do you understand that?" No, and I thank God I don't understand it for the Bible says, "And without controversy great is the mystery of godliness" (1 Tim. 3:16). God was manifest in the flesh and I'm so grateful that the virgin birth of Jesus Christ does not depend upon your understanding nor my understanding for its validation. I wouldn't have any confidence in a God I could understand.

Vance Havner has said, "I don't understand electricity but I don't intend to sit around in the dark until I do." My friend, I could not explain the mystery of the virgin birth any more than I could explain Almighty God. Beloved friend, never try to explain miracles. Just say, "I believe in God. I believe in God!" Isn't it a biological impossibility that a virgin could conceive? My friend, let an angel answer that. Luke 1:37, "But with God all things are possible." *With God.*

You know, some people try to explain miracles. People move heaven and earth trying to find fish big enough to swallow a man and keep him alive for three days and three nights and they say, "Oh, there's a certain shark over here that could do it. There's a certain whale over here." That doesn't make any difference. We are dealing with God. You don't have to try to explain it. You don't have to help God. If God wanted to, He could create a fish with five rooms of furniture and a refrigerator. He has no difficulty doing that. With God all things are possible.

Dr. Lee Scarborough, at one time president of Southwestern Seminary in Texas, was preaching on the story of Jonah and the whale. When he got home, his son said to him, "Daddy, did you really mean what you preached? Do you really believe that? Daddy, do you believe that a fish could swallow a man and keep him alive for three days and three nights?"

This great man sat his son down and said, "Well now son, let me ask you a question. If God could make a man to begin with out of absolutely nothing and if God could make a fish to begin with out of absolutely nothing, son, don't you believe that God could make a fish that could keep a man alive for three days and three nights?"

The little fellow said, "Well, if you're going to bring God into it that's different."

Friend, if you don't mind, I'd just like to bring God into the virgin birth. I believe in the virgin birth.

The late, great Robert G. Lee said this:

I don't believe that God is an impotent and puzzled bellhop running up and down the corridors of the house He designed by His omniscience and created by His omnipotence, having lost the key to some of the mystery rooms of His own house. It is impossible for Him to be baffled or bothered or chained by the physical elements.

Now there is a third thing I want you to notice—not only the sinful mockery of the virgin birth, not only the sacred mystery of His birth, but what I'm going to call the sovereign majesty of His birth. The angel said in Luke 1:32-33 speaking of this child that shall be born,

And he shall be great and shall be called the Son of the Highest; and the Lord God shall give unto him the throne of his father David: And he shall reign over the house of Jacob for ever; and of his kingdom there shall be no end.

Praise the Lord for the sovereign majesty of His birth.

This child which was born was God in human flesh. God was His Father and like Father, like Son. Hebrews 1:8, "But unto the Son he saith, Thy throne, O God, is for ever and ever: a sceptre of righteousness is the sceptre of thy kingdom."

When the prophet Isaiah spoke of this so long ago, he said, "Unto us a child is born," and that spoke of His humanity. But then he said, "Unto us a son is given." That spoke of His deity for this Babe of Bethlehem was the earthly child of a Heavenly Father and the Heavenly Child of an earthly mother. He was fully God. He was as much God as though He were not man at all but He was as much man as though He were not God at all. He was not all God and no man, He was not all man and no God, He was not half God and half man. He was fully God and fully man. He was the God-man. There was never another like Him.

I want to tell you something. That little baby of Luke 2 was the mighty God of Genesis 1. He is the Word that spoke the universe into existence. Billions of suns, planets, and stars flew from His fingertips, oceans dripped from His fingers, He was the One that scooped out the seas, heaped up the mountains, flung out the sun, moon, and stars. Hallelujah for such a Savior!

And the Bible says, "And the word was made flesh and dwelt among us." What is a "word"? A "word" is an expression of an invisible idea. Jesus Christ is the Expression of the invisible God and John Philipps has rightly said,

> The great mystery of the manger is that God should be able to translate deity into humanity without even discarding the deity or distorting the humanity. He is fully God and He is forever God.

Jesus Christ did not have His beginning in Bethlehem. He did not have His beginning in maternity, but in eternity. He did not begin with Mary, He began in the bosom of the Father and never ever really began. I want to tell you, when Jesus Christ was born, He was as old as His Father and older than His mother. Jesus Christ is forever God.

I had the privilege and the responsibility of spending several hours witnessing to Muhammed Ali. We had quite a Bible discussion. He said, "I want to ask you a question. You say that Jesus Christ is the Son of God because He was born of a virgin.

Adam didn't have either a father or a mother. Wouldn't that make Adam even more a Son of God than Jesus Christ?" I said, "Champ, let me tell you something. Jesus Christ was not the Son of God because He was born of a virgin. He was born of a virgin because He was the Son of God and we need to understand this." He is the sovereign God. Thank God He was born to reign and to rule and the Bible says He is going to rule over the throne of His Father David.

I tell you, you're looking at one preacher who believes in the earthly reign of Jesus Christ Who is coming again. I believe with all my heart that Jesus shall reign. One of these days those dimpled little feet that lay upon that manger straw will be the nail-pierced feet that will touch the Mount of Olives and the earth will heave with an earthquake when Jesus comes to rule and to reign. Thank God for the sovereign majesty of His birth.

People are trying to figure it out. What are we going to do? The U.N. meets, the diplomats huddle together, they plan for peace and the world is in pieces. China's operational head said recently to the president of the United States, "Mankind is indisputedly headed for world war." Alexander Solzhenitsyn, that brilliant Russian dissident, said this: "It is too late to avoid the third World War." The late Albert Schweitzer said, "Man has lost his capacity to foresee and forestall. He will end by destroying the earth." H. G. Wells, the historian who lived only one year into the atomic age said, "For man and his world, there is no way out and all people have the idea we are looking into the muzzle of a loaded cannon."

Are you listening to me? Dear friend, the only hope for planet earth is the coming again of Bethlehem's Babe. I believe that with all of my heart, with all of my soul. When the angel said, "Peace on earth," that same angel said, "He shall reign on the throne of His Father David." Hallelujah—the cradle, the cross, and the crown are inseparably linked!

Let me say one last word. Let me think with you not only about the sinful mockery of His birth, the sacred mystery of His birth, and the sovereign majesty of His birth but Oh, thank God, let me talk about the saving ministry of His birth. "For the angel said, you shall call His name Jesus and He shall save His people from their sin. For unto you is born this day in the city of David, a Savior which is Christ the Lord." Now listen to me my friend, I said at the introduction of this message, without the virgin birth, I would not give you half a hallelujah for your hope of heaven.

Let me explain why I said that. There must be a blood atonement for sin. There must be a blood atonement for sin. There must be. The Bible says in Leviticus 17:11, "It is the blood that maketh atonement for the soul." The Bible says in Hebrews 9:22, "Without shedding of blood, there is no remission." God will never overlook sin. "The wages of sin is death, the life of the flesh is the blood thereof." That blood must be shed is an atonement for sin. I for one believe in that old-fashioned doctrine of the blood atonement, the substitutionary blood atonement.

God cannot overlook sin. If God would overlook sin, He would cease to be a holy God. The crowning attribute of Almighty God is not love, though He is infinite love. If you had to take one word and crystallize the character of God into one word, and thank God we don't, but if we had to take all the lexicons of the world and find one word that would describe the character of God, in my opinion, that one word would have to be *holy*. Holy, holy, holy is the Lord God of hosts. Holy is the Father. Holy is the Son. Holy is the Spirit of God. And that word "holy" means that God is the complete other, He is the antithesis, He is the opposite of sin. He has a holy hatred for sin. God is sworn by His holiness that sin must be punished. If God were to fail to punish sin, God would fail to be holy.

They say in a courtroom that when a guilty man is acquitted, the judge is condemned. If the Judge of the Supreme Court of the Universe were to allow sin to go unpunished, God Himself would become a sinner. God would topple from His throne of holiness. God has said that sin must be punished. Therefore we need someone to become the substitute. But who can he be? That blood must be worthy blood, that blood must be innocent blood. Are you listening to me? Here is the why of the virgin birth. No son of Adam could ever qualify. I'll tell you why. Romans 5:12 says, "Wherefore as by one man sin entered into the world and death by sin." And then again the Bible says, "In Adam all die" (1 Cor. 15:22a).

But notice what it says. "By one man sin entered into the world." Listen, the Bible teaches there was one man named Adam and the Bible teaches there was a woman named Eve. I reject with all the umption and emotion of my soul that monkey mythology that man evolved. I believe in the direct creation of Adam and Eve.

We have some telling us today that it really doesn't make any difference whether we believe in Adam and Eve, that a part of our great diversity is not to believe there was one man and one woman who was the mother of us all. But the Bible says, "For by one man's disobedience many were made sinners, by another man's obedience many are made righteous" (Rom. 5:19), and, "as in Adam all die. Even so, in Christ shall all be made alive" 1 Cor. 15:22. Listen and listen well. If Genesis 3 is a myth, John 3 is a farce. If Genesis 3 is a myth, people don't need a birth from above, all we need is a boost from below. I mean, we just need to keep on progressing. But dear friend,

Adam and no son of Adam could ever die on the cross for my sins.

Do you know what determines the bloodline? Do you know what determines the blood of that embryo, that fetus, that baby in its mother's womb? The father determines that. None of the blood of that baby carried in the womb circulates in the mother's body. As a matter of fact, the child may have one blood type and the mother may have an entirely different blood type. You know that don't you? Who determines the blood? It is the father who determines the blood. What blood was in the Lord Jesus Christ? The blood of God!

Now somebody says, "Wait a minute. Wait a minute. God doesn't have blood." He did when Jesus was here. You say, "Adrian, that's silly." You think it's silly? Listen to this verse. Acts 20:28:

> Take heed therefore unto yourselves, and to all the flock, over which the Holy Ghost hath made you overseers, to feed the church of God, which he hath purchased with his own blood.

I want to tell you, that crimson flow that fell at Calvary was the blood of God. The blood of God was shed on that cross.

Why was Jesus born of a virgin? He came as He did virgin-born to be what He was . . . the God-man. He was what He was, the God-man, to do what He did—die as a substitute. He did what He did that He might change what I was. Praise His Holy Name. Jesus was born of a virgin that you might be born again. Jesus became the Son of Man that we might become the sons of God. Jesus came to earth that we might go to heaven and without the virgin birth it was absolutely, totally impossible.

I want to tell you something that happened to me the day

before yesterday. As I was coming to Atlanta on the airplane, I sat by a teenage girl. My seat had been changed and I asked a lady if she would mind changing places with me as I wanted to sit by my wife. The lady was kind so I was really sitting in the wrong seat as this young lady came and sat down beside me and buckled in. She was fifteen years of age. I looked over at her and she looked so lonely. After a while I turned and began a conversation with her.

I said, "How are you?"

"Fine."

"Are you going on vacation?"

She said, "I'm going to visit my aunt."

I said, "How long are you going to stay?"

She said, "Well, about six weeks. I'm going to spend the summer. I'm going to work, try to earn some money."

I said, "Let me ask you a question. Have you been thinking about giving your heart to Jesus? Have you been thinking about being saved?"

She looked at me and said, "Mister, I want to ask you a question. Is suicide a sin?"

I said, "Little lady, yes, suicide is a sin. But you don't have to think of suicide because Jesus said, 'I'm come that you might have life and have it more abundantly.'"

I took the Word of God and began to share with her from the Word of God. She told me how her stepfather (she was from a broken home) was an alcoholic. She told me how the aunt whom she hardly knew was a drunkard. She poured out a little bit of the disappointment and the heartache of her life and I shared with her how Jesus, the virgin-born Son of God who is the Savior, died for her sin and how much God loved her.

I said, "Little lady, wouldn't you like to be saved right here on this airplane? Would you allow me to lead you in a prayer and you can receive Christ as your personal Savior?"

She said, "Yes, very much." There on that airplane we prayed and she opened her sweet little heart. She gave her heart to Jesus Christ and she was wondrously saved—born again!

I got to thinking about that later on and, listen, I believe that what happened on that airplane the day before yesterday was a greater miracle than the virgin birth of Christ. Now pay attention. I believe that the New Birth is a greater miracle than the virgin birth. I believe that it took more of God's love and grace to save that girl than it did even to send His Son. Let me tell you something. Jesus died in agony and blood upon the cross.

One man asked his pastor, "Pastor, do you believe there is life on other planets?" The pastor said, "No, I really don't believe there is." And he said, "Well, why did God go to all that trouble to make those planets?" He said, "What trouble? I mean, God spoke and it was so." The creation was no trouble for God. The virgin birth was no trouble for God.

The only time God ever went to trouble was Calvary, where His Son hung and bled in ignominious shame. It took the blood of Jesus Christ, that virgin-born Lamb, to save that little girl. I'm going to tell you something else. The angel Gabriel came to Mary and announced the virgin birth. But the angel Gabriel can never lead a soul to Jesus Christ. What happened on that airplane yesterday—and I'm not minimizing the virgin birth and it never would have happened without the virgin birth—but the new birth is a greater miracle than the virgin birth.

Let Congress run the nation. Let Wall Street handle the finances. Let the president make the decisions. Let Hollywood have the fame. Just let me be a winner of souls. Thank God for the saving ministry of His birth. Hallelujah! No virgin birth, no Deity; no Deity, no sinlessness; no sinlessness, no atonement; not atonement, no hope. Thank God for the virgin birth!

5
Jesus Christ: the Same Yesterday, Today, and Forever

by Jay Strack

Jay Strack

Jay Strack, a native of Orlando, Florida, is an evangelist from Fort Myers, Florida. He heads the Jay Strack Evangelistic Association. He has also pastored the Riverside Baptist Church, Fort Myers, for four years in the past. He holds the master's and doctor's degrees from Luther Rice Theological Seminary. He has authored many pamphlets and articles on drugs and alcohol and books, *Drugs and Drinking: What Every Teen and Parent Should Know* and *The Transformer*, books on crises facing young people. His family includes his wife, the former Diane Raso, and two daughters, Lisa and Christa.

5

Jesus Christ: the Same Yesterday, Today, and Forever

by Jay Strack

In Hebrews 13:5-8, the Bible states,

Let your conversation be without covetousness; and be content with such things as ye have: for he hath said, I will never leave thee, nor forsake thee. So that we may boldly say, The Lord is my helper, and I will not fear what man shall do unto me. Remember them which have the rule over you, who have spoken unto you the word of God: who faith follow, considering the end of their conversation. Jesus Christ the same yesterday, and today, and for ever.

Several months ago I was in a crusade and I got a phone call from my wife. She was very, very troubled and even though she tried to disguise her mood, I could tell something was troubling her. Finally I asked her, "Honey, what's the problem?" She does what most wives do when we are away and they don't want to trouble us with what's going on. Finally she told me. We were preparing for a move and she was cleaning out several boxes of books. In one box she found books by three different preachers who have been very prominent with the hand of God on their lives. They had preached with power and had seen decisions, but these three preachers whose names she ran across in one box no longer were in the ministry. As a young wife and the wife of a young evangelist, she said with tears over the phone, "Honey, let's resolve in our hearts that we will cross the finish line for Jesus."

I've never been able to escape that phrase and so as I preach to brothers and sisters today, "I want you to know that it is God's Will that as His people we cross the finish line." A faith that fizzles out before the finish, I believe, was faulty from the very first. I believe it is possible to keep your eyes on Jesus as you run the race.

When I preach in high-school auditoriums and football stadiums across the country, I try to teach teenagers, moms, and dads that this Book is God's Word. They can build their lives on it; they can build their future on it. You can trust the Word of God in this generation of scoffers.

In Hebrews 12, verses 1-3 the Bible says,

> Wherefore, seeing we also are compassed about with so great a cloud of witnesses, let us lay aside every weight, and the sin which doth so easily beset us, and let us run with patience the race that is set before us. Looking unto Jesus the author and finisher of our faith; who for the joy that was set before him endureth the cross, despising the shame, and is set down at the right hand of the throne of God. For consider him that endureth such contradiction of sinners against himself, lest ye be wearied and faint in your minds.

I have been told that the statistics among pastors who are dropping out of the ministry either voluntarily or involuntarily are staggering. If you will take it from a young man who is now an evangelist but who had the privilege of being a pastor, may I say that it takes more anointing to be a godly, Spirit-filled pastor, shepherding day by day than it does to preach to thirty-thousand people in a stadium. I know that if you are the shepherd God has called you to be, you cannot help but be weary and discouraged. The purpose of my message, and God knows my heart, is to encourage you and to encourage myself for His sake, for our families' sake, for the world's sake, to cross the finish line.

I would like for you to jot down what I believe are several motivational factors for us to cross the finish line. First of all, I  want you to notice our predecessors in the faith. One of the things that encourages me is that I know there are many who have gone before me, that they have run the race. The Bible says in Hebrews 12:1, "Wherefore, seeing we also are encompassed about with so great a cloud of witnesses." Now where in the world is this crowd of witnesses and who are they? The Bible tells us in Hebrews 11 the cloud of witnesses are the men and women of God that have lived for God before us.

In Hebrews 11:3, the Bible says, "Through faith we understand that the worlds were framed by the word of God, so that things which are seen were not made of things which do appear." The Bible tells us we can have faith in the living God because He is a God of creation. But notice verse 4. "By faith Abel offered unto God a more excellent sacrifice than Cain, by which he obtained witness that he was righteous, God testifying of his gifts: and by it he being dead yet speaketh." My dear friend, if there were not an Adam and an Eve literally, there could not have been a literal Cain and Abel and I want you to know, "By faith Abel offered unto God."

So the Bible says I must have faith in creation. The Bible says

I can learn by the example of Abel. It says in verse 6, "But without faith it is impossible to please him: for he that cometh to God must believe that he is, and that he is a rewarder of them that diligently seek Him."

How many times does the global judgment of God in the days of Noah come under attack and question? "By faith Noah, being warned of God of things not seen as yet, moved with fear, prepared an ark to the saving of his house; by which he condemned the world, and became heir of the righteousness which is by faith" (Heb. 11:7). Now look at verse 29. The Bible says we are to have the faith of Moses. "By faith they passed through the Red Sea as by dry land; which the Egyptians assaying to do were drowned." I want to share with you, it's no concidence that Satan himself has attacked the Word of God to undermine the very examples that will speak to men and women of God.

The people of Hebrews 11 walked by faith and God wants us to know there is no other way. When we are weary, discouraged and brokenhearted, God has demonstrated through the example of others that the way to overcome our heartaches is by faith. I want to tell you something. I came to the place in my young life as a college student when I had to simply say, "God, I trust Your Word and if You give me an example in Your Word, I'm going to live it. I'm going to live by faith. I'm going to please You and I don't want to please anybody else."

In verse 33, we read, "Who through faith subdued kingdoms, wrought righteousness, obtained promises, stopped the mouths of lions, Quenched the violence of fire." I'm reminded of Polycarp when the Romans said to him, "If you do not confess that Caesar is lord, we will burn you at the stake." Polycarp looked at those men of political power and said, "You will burn my body with flames that last for just a few hours but there is a God of judgment that has a flame that will burn forever and if you don't turn from your sin, you will feel that flame." They wanted to nail Polycarp to the stake and he said, "No, the same power that kept my blessed Lord Jesus on the cross will give me power to stand at the stake." Polycarp went to his death in the flames of persecution singing, "Thank You Lord for counting me worthy to die for You."

So the Bible talks about those who have stopped the mouths of lions and quenched the violence of fire, those that have escaped the edge of the sword, those out of weakness who were made strong, those who waxed valiant in flight and turned to flight the armies of the aliens. Women received their dead raised to life again: and others were tortured.

Look at verse 36.

And others had trial of cruel mockings and scourgings, yea, moreover of bonds and imprisonment: They were stoned, they were sawn asunder, were tempted, were slain with the sword: they wandered about in sheepskins and goatskins; being destitute, afflicted, tormented. Of whom the world was not worthy: they wandered in deserts, and in mountains, and in dens and caves of the earth.

One of the things that motivates me whenever I become tired, discouraged, or weary is to remember that others have already finished the race. There are those who have gone before you, those that so loved the Lord and were so full of His Spirit they counted their life as nothing in order to make a stand for Him. Oh, our predecessors in the faith!

When I look at this commitment, I notice some had a trial of mockings. Yet I saw a church newsletter where a pastor had complimented his members for braving the rain. Think about that a moment. Do you know they actually ran to their car and probably got a little wet and then they had to drive through the rain with windshield wipers. They had to park as close as they could to the front door as their wives and children hurried into the building. Can you imagine, dad had to park half a block away and dad got wet!

I don't know about you, but when I read about how those dear Christians braved the rain, I called my staff together. I could hardly hold back the tears. I wanted to open my Bible to Hebrews, chapter 11 and read, "And they were stoned and cut in two and tempted and slain with the sword." I was tempted to write in the margin, "and they braved the rain." I want to tell you, something is wrong with the level of commitment in our generation.

Well, the Bible talks about the predecessors in the race. But notice the Bible also talks about our preparation for the race. It says in verse 1, ". . . let us lay aside every weight, and the sin which doth so easily beset us." The Bible says we've got to prepare to run the race. You see, the Bible says we've got to lay aside anything in our lives that will slow us down. There are many things in our lives that are going to slow us down from crossing the finish line. There is excess weight. Some of us are caught up in materialism, some of us are caught up in pleasing men more than pleasing God. Now I can't be the Holy Spirit in your life but I believe the Spirit of God will speak to some who are in financial bondage, some who have your minds on so many other things. It's no wonder you keep stumbling in the race. The Bible says, ". . . lay aside everything in your life that will slow you down."

But notice it also says, ". . . and cast away that one sin." A definite article is used to speak of the sin which doth so easily beset us. There is, I'm convinced, often one sin which Satan will use as a stronghold in your life. It may be carnality. It may be immorality. It may be secret habits. It may be appetites. But I want to share something with you. I read this and Oh, God, I want to cross the finish line. I don't want to be one of those stars that burn bright for a little while and then fall to the ground. I want my life to count for God. From time to time God has shown me areas of my life that were weighing me down and taking my mind off the things of God and the calling of God.

Brothers and sisters, cast aside the sin in your life. You know what it is. The Spirit of God will make it very obvious. Satan often uses one thing to trip us up. The Bible says there must be preparation for the race. If you want to run the race and finish the race, you must cast off this excess stuff in your life which is keeping you from being like Jesus. Remember the old song, "Let Others See Jesus in You." I believe there's enough sin in most of our lives that will keep people from seeing Jesus Christ in us. But only holy men and women of God can do the business of a Holy God. Carnal people, no matter how hard they try, will accomplish nothing.

The Bible says, "Run the race." I can't speak for you but I've had the privilege of being with enough men of God across the country that I know many of you have the same prayer I do. I want it to be said of me what was said of Elijah when the lady said, "I perceive that a holy man of God passes by us continuously." I want to be that holy man of God. I want to prepare to run the race. There was a pastor who fell into immorality. He stumbled in sin. He lost his ministry and he lost his family. I said to him, "We've been friends a long time. Tell me. I want to know what you're going through. I want to know how you feel." I never will forget hearing his answer. He said, "You know, I feel like the fallen angel in hell. It's not the flames so much, but I miss the sound of the trumpet in the morning." We must hear the trumpet of God in the morning to be prepared for the race.

The Bible says we have predecessors in the race. The Bible says there must be preparation for the race. Then the Bible talks about our participation in the race. The time has come to get off the fence. The time has come for some of us to make those commitments in our hearts to be God's men and to be God's women. You see, the Bible says we can't just be a spectator. You know, the Super Bowl has been described as ninety-thousand people in a stadium and millions via television watching twenty-two men on the field. You have millions of people in desperate need of exercising watching twenty-two men in desperate need of rest. That's the Super Bowl and I'm going to tell you something, the Bible says we must participate in the race.

First of all, notice the pace of this race. The Bible says, "let us run." Do you know something? The Bible says the race God has called you to is not a sprint. It's not a hundred-yard dash nor relay race. It breaks my heart to know that many folks cast their church letters out the window when they move. You see, that's not snow on the top of the Rocky Mountains, the Blue Ridge Mountains, or the Smoky Mountains—those are church letters. I've got news for you, friend. Life is not a sprint, it's not a hundred-yard dash, nor is it a relay race. We don't have the option to say, "I'm getting tired. It's your turn to run, you take it from here." You will pass the torch on to somebody else only when Jesus takes you home.

The Bible says to run the race at a certain pace. The Bible says we must run with patience. That word is often translated "endurance." Also, the Bible says it is a predetermined race. The race that is set before us. We must be careful not to fall into the trap of comparing our ministry to others. There are many times when we say, "You know, I wish I had that man's ministry. That man's got more influence than I have. God's got His hand on that man more than on me." Sometimes without realizing it, we become covetous. But you will never know real joy, you will never finish the race if you try to run the race God has called others to run.

The Bible says there is a predetermined race. You are to run that race that is set before you. I once said, "You know, if I could just pastor, then I could be home every night with my family." Now that tells you I had to have a drug flashback to ever believe that. I became a pastor and I don't think I hardly ever had a night at home with my family. Please take it from a young man who used to mow lawns in the summertime, if the grass looks greener in somebody else's yard, it's normally over a septic tank. Have you ever noticed that? I want you to understand, the grass may look greener but it needs mowing a lot more often. The Bible says run the race that is set before you.

And then the Bible says in Hebrews 12:2, "Looking unto Jesus the author and finisher of our faith." God's Word speaks of our perception as we run the race. Please hear this. There are no minor prophets. And when God has called you and you are God's man attempting to run the race, "look unto Jesus." That phrase means "look away from everything else and from everyone else and fix your eyes on Him."

I thank God that Southern Baptists believe in the priesthood of the believer. If I read my Bible correctly, I notice that the priest always loved the prophets and the priests desired a word from the prophets. With all my heart I believe the greatest need in America today is for the prophetic voices of God to herald the Good News that "Jesus Saves." When God's hand is upon you, don't doubt in darkness what God reveals plainly to you in light. Don't ever ask, "What will this profit me if I preach this way or if I take this position or if I do this or if I don't do that?"

Hear me, men of God. We'll sacrifice the opportunity to be the prophets of God if we seek human applause more than heavenly applause. Do you know why so many people are tripped up as they run the race? Because they've got their eyes on everyone else. They've got their eyes on those beside them. Do you wait to see what the Gallup Poll says before you make a decision about speaking against the sin of homosexuality or the sin of abortion? Listen friend, I don't care what the Gallup Poll says. I'm going to preach what God says to preach to the best of my ability. I'm going to preach it in love, I want to be full of grace, but I must be full of grace *and* truth. You'll never finish the race if you've got an eye on the bleachers. You'll never finish the race if you are seeking human applause. It's only when you seek the applause of heaven that you can be the prophet of God.

The greatest need in America today is for men of God to say, "Oh God, the job is so great, the demands are so great, the pressure is such that there is no way I can do it. You've got to breath on me, you've got to give me the message. O God, you've got to give me the power. I can't make it." When we are weak enough, we fall on our knees before our Holy Heavenly Father but then the Bible says when God breathes upon us, we are able to stand up, thunder forth, "thus saith the Lord." I thank God that all I've got to do is please Him rather than pleasing anybody else. People sometimes encourage me to stay in the "mainstream" and preach in such a manner as to be acceptable to everybody. You know the stream I want to be in? It is the same stream John the Baptist was in when he waded in and began to preach repentance. It's the same stream Jesus was in when the Father spoke from heaven and said, "This is my beloved Son in whom I'm well pleased." I pray that the mainstream of life will be that of repentance, that of pleasing God.

Do you know one of the reasons that motivates me to finish the race? The Bible says, "looking unto Jesus." I know that Jesus is waiting for me. The Author and the Finisher, the One who fires the gun and begins the race, the One who waits for me to wave the flag at the finish line. Our Commencer in the race is our Congratulator at the end of the race.

But do you know something else? He's also our Companion during the race. Do you know why in Hebrews 11 they were able to stop the mouths of lions and stand the flames of persecution? Jesus Christ was there with them. As we run the race, looking unto Jesus, the Bible says He's running the race at our side. When I run and I know that He runs with me and that I'm running His race, it gives me courage and motivation to finish the race.

I had motivation yesterday to finish the race. I had the privilege of preaching in an Atlanta church and a young man walked up to me and said, "Do you recognize me?" I said, "To be honest with you, I really don't." He told me his name and I remembered. His name was Lee. The last time I saw Lee he had hair down to shoulders and about seven earrings in his ear and he was stoned out of his mind, rebelling, and breaking the heart of his family. Lee came forward one night after the Word of God was preached, hope was offered, and repentance was stressed. Lee gave his heart and life to Jesus. I stood looking into the eyes of a young man, clean-cut, wearing a three-piece suit with a tie clip that said, "Jesus Saves." He said, "God's called me to the ministry." Then a man made his way through the crowd and cried like a baby. He said, "Jay, this is our son, Lee. Once he was dead but now he's alive. This is our son. He was lost but now he's found." That's why we must finish the race. That's why we can't stop. That's why we must continue.

I was in Vicksburg, Mississippi, in an area-wide crusade and a young lady came up to me with tears streaming down her face. She said, "I heard you speak in Vicksburg High School and I came tonight wanting to be saved but my boyfriend talked me out of being saved tonight but he's promised he'd come with me tomorrow night." Tuesday night came . . . she didn't come forward. Wednesday night came . . . she didn't come forward. Thursday night came and this young lady walked down the aisle and tapped me on the shoulder and she said, "Preacher, I'm the young lady who talked to you Sunday. I'm coming tonight to give my life to Christ."

I saw her later in the counseling area. She said, "Jay, I'm pregnant and Saturday my boyfriend was driving me to Jackson, Mississippi, to have an abortion but I've been saved. I've been forgiven. You said God would make me brand-new if I would trust Him." I watched a beautiful young lady— pregnant, at the lowest point of her life, feeling like nobody cared for her, thinking thoughts of suicide, on her way soon to have an abortion—changed by the gospel of the Lord Jesus Christ. He cleansed her, forgave her, and made her brand-new. When I saw that young lady, she had the glow of God on her face and she knew it was God's will for her to have that baby, put that baby up for adoption, and make sure her life was pleasing God.

That's what we are all about. We've prayed, worked, and worked that someday Southern Baptists would be big enough and strong enough to change the world. We can, but only if we run the race. We can't get discouraged. We can't get weary, we can't quit. We must keep running.

I believe with all my heart Jesus Christ is counting on me. If you don't believe He is counting on you there is something not right in your walk with Him. I sense He's counting on me. My little girl became separated from my wife and me in one of the largest malls in the state of Florida. We don't really know how it happened but we looked up, my wife thought she was with me and I thought she was with my wife. My oldest little girl, Melissa, got separated from us for fifteen to twenty minutes in one of the largest malls in the state. The night before my wife and I had watched the special on Adam Walsh. Perhaps you know the story. The young boy became lost in the mall in Florida and they found him later, decapitated.

Now all of a sudden here's our little girl lost in this large mall, and I'm ashamed to tell you we thought the worse. We began to panic. I rushed outside and began to run around the parking lot for fear that somebody might be trying to get my little girl into a car. Then I ran through the mall. I didn't worry what people thought about me. I didn't worry about how dignified I was. I didn't worry about the tears running down my face. My wife didn't worry about the makeup running down her face. We were frantic. During the twenty minutes we ran and searched for our little girl. They seemed like the longest twenty minutes in our lives.

Finally we heard some of the sweetest words in all the world. We heard on the intercom, "We understand the parents of Melissa Strack are lost." Our little girl had gone and said, "My mom and dad are lost. Would you find them?" I ran and grabbed my little girl . . . I didn't know whether to hug her or spank her. But as we rejoiced and wept, I looked at my little girl and I said, "Melissa, were you afraid? Honey, were you sacred? Honey, what in the world were you thinking about?"

She said, "I wasn't afraid. I wasn't scared at all." A few minutes later as we walked down the mall, I was holding her in my arms and she said, "Do you know why, Dad? I was counting on you. I was counting on you to find me."

I want to tell you something. I have two little girls counting on their daddy to live a godly life, to live a holy life, to cross the finish line, to not give in to flirtation, to not get up pleasing man, to not get caught up after money. I've got two little girls who are counting on their daddy to be real so they will know what God is all about. I've got not only my little girls counting on me, I believe I've got the Lord Jesus Christ counting on me. When I get to heaven I want the Lord Jesus Christ to say to me, "Jay, well done thou good and faithful servant. I was counting on you."

This story illustrates how Jesus is counting on us. Someone imagined that when Jesus went back to heaven, the Father looked at Jesus after His death on the cross and said, "Well, is it accomplished?" And Jesus said, "It is accomplished." The Father said, "What have you done?" Jesus said, "I put in the hands of twelve men the future of mankind. And then in the years through the years, there will be a denomination called Southern Baptists and I put in their hands the responsibility to tell every man, woman, and child about Me." And the Father said to Jesus, "What if Southern Baptists don't do it?" And Jesus said, "They have to do it. I'm counting on them."

Hear me, pastor. No matter where you're serving, He's counting on you. We better do the work of God. We better be faithful, fight the fights and keep the faith, for Jesus is the same yesterday, today, and forever!

6
Looking to Jesus at All Times

By Harry Garvin

Harry B. Garvin

Harry B. Garvin, a native of Anson, Texas, was appointed to serve as a missionary in Uganda in 1969 and has continued to serve there ever since. Formerly he was pastor of the Dixie Heights Baptist Church, Fort Worth, Texas. He holds the B.S. degree from Howard Payne University, Brownwood, Texas, and the B.D. degree from Southwestern Baptist Theological Seminary. He is married to the former Doris Shott of Hamby, Texas. They have six children, four of them now adults. Rebecca and Angie are still at home.

6
Looking to Jesus at All Times

by Harry Garvin

Several years ago I was in the bush, maybe forty miles from where I live, ten miles from the nearest road. We were opening a new church. We had a mud house with a grass roof and wooden windows. There was a blind woman in that church. After we had worshipped some three to four hours, even killing a spitting cobra in the midst of the worship, that blind woman stood outside as we were about to say goodbye. She began to clap her hands and to sing. This is what she was singing in her native language: "I am so happy with Jesus, my Savior. Let us all go to see Him, let us all go to heaven. I'm so happy that I can go to heaven and see the Lord."

She's always blessed me and I have remembered her for so many years. We are speaking of looking to Jesus, looking to Jesus at all times. Hebrews 11:36 to 12:1 says,

And others experienced mockings and scourgings, yes, also chains and imprisonment. They were stoned, they were put to death with the sword, they were tempted, they went about in sheep skins and goat skins, they were destitute, afflicted, ill-treated (men of whom the world was not worthy), wandering in deserts and mountains and caves and holes in the ground and in all these, having gained approval through their faith, they did not receive what was promised because God had provided something better for us, so that apart from us they should not be made perfect. Therefore, since we have so great a cloud of witnesses surrounding us, let us lay aside every encumbrance and the sin which so easily entangles us [Could that be leaving our first love, the love of bringing men to Christ?] . . . and let us run with endurance the race that is set before us (NASB).

I like the *New American Standard* translation of verse 2: "fixing our eyes on Jesus, the author and perfector of faith." Fixing our eyes on Jesus. Paul said to Timothy, "be instant in season, out of season" (2 Tim. 4:2). He was saying, "No matter how tough it gets, whether it's easy or whether it's difficult, fix your eyes on Jesus and be faithful. Stay with the job. No one might ever know your name, they might not know the name of your church, but fix your eyes on Jesus and move forward."

Doris and I were called to missions under the ministry of Baker James Cauthen in 1962. We hoped to be overseas in '66. There was hepatitus. I was ill and not well for almost three years. We didn't make it in 1966. We thought we would be appointed in 1968. My wife became ill with a disintegrating disc in her back and the Foreign Mission Board said, "We don't believe you can go with a radical change in your wife's back. You cannot go as a foreign missionary." We did not get angry but we looked to Jesus.

My wife, who is very timid, at that time could hardly stand in front of a small group. She said, "Harry, God wants to heal my back. I want to share my testimony with our church [Dixie Heights Baptist Church in Fort Worth] and ask them if they will pray with me. James said, 'the prayer of faith will heal the sick'" (Jas. 5:15). So my wife gave her testimony and she looked to Jesus and those people in that congregation looked to Jesus and were stirred in their hearts as they came forward almost to the person to lay their hands upon her and God healed her back and we made it to Uganda in 1970. Looking to Jesus.

We got to Uganda just in time to meet Idi Amin who ruled Uganda for almost nine years. He was a wicked man, a diabolical man, perhaps possessed of evil spirits of Satan. I know that man. I shook his hand on one occasion. That man caused so much chaos and confusion. One day twenty-seven bodies were dumped at the source where the water pipe sucked up the water to take it to the town where we lived. We had always boiled our water. I can tell you we boiled our water a lot longer after that. People were suffering. Things were difficult. It was not an easy time in '72 and '73—they were very hard.

One morning, as was my custom, I was up before sunup. I was praying and having my quiet time—looking to Jesus. I was deeply troubled in my heart. A friend had phoned me from Kenya and said, "Harry, you are stubborn and you are a fool. Get out of Uganda or you and your children will lose your lives." I wondered if I were making a mistake. I knew I was stubborn. I didn't think I was a fool. I prayed, "Oh, God, show us what to do." I prayed. We all prayed.

As I was reading that morning in Daniel, I read about Shadrach, Meshach, and Abednego. They were thrown into the fiery furnace, taken out, and the smell of fire was not even upon them. I continued reading. I read about Daniel. He refused to quit. He was faithful to Jehovah God and, because of his faithfulness, he was not awarded a new car as many pastors are, he was not awarded a fancy home as some pastors are, he was not awarded anything that was easy. He was thrown into the lions' den. He was placed in jeopardy.

As I read Hebrews 11, I find that following Jesus does not

mean that you will be counted a success always as the world counts success. There is so much suffering in the church of Jesus Christ across the world and there is that part of maturity that can never be known without suffering. Jesus learned maturity through suffering and the church of Jesus Christ will mature through suffering. If you've not had suffering, something about you is lacking. You need to experience some suffering in your life to be mature for our Lord Jesus Christ.

There at that point, Daniel was thrown into the lions' den. But the next morning Nebuchadnezzar found him all right. The lions had shut their mouths at the instigation of the angel and they were unable to harm him. Those were healthy, hungry lions because they ate up the next bunch of people who were thrown into that den.

There I was praying and reading the Bible. I remember bowing my head at my desk and suddenly, I cannot describe what happened. It was—how can I say it?—like an electric blanket wrapped around me from head to foot. There was the glorious electricity of the Holy Spirit. There was the saturation of the presence of Almighty God and there as I wept and the tears flowed upon my desk, I became aware of the all-powerful God that we serve and God spoke to me. Deep in my heart, in my being, there was the voice of God and here's what He said: "Harry, the question is not staying in Uganda and suffering, or going out of Uganda and not suffering. The question is My Will. The safest place on the earth is in My Will. Shadrach, Meshach, and Abednego belong to Me. I protected them in the burning furnace. I protected Daniel in the lions' den and, if I choose, I can protect you."

The question is not living or dying, the question is the Will of God for my life. I'm here to tell you if we worry about dying we cannot win the world to Christ. If we worry about suffering we cannot win the world for our Jesus. We must look to Jesus at all times and be willing to suffer if God calls us to suffer. You can die in the Will of God. Christians have died in the Will of God through the centuries and will continue to do so. But what's bad about that? If you die in the Will of God, praise God, you go to heaven. Are you afraid to go to heaven?

They were vicious. They drove a certain kind of car. I knew who they were. We were getting ready for a Sunday evening worship service in my house and four of these men came into my house and said, "We know that you are here illegally. You're a spy." This was in 1975. I knew they were going to arrest me. They said, "We want to know what you are teaching. Where is your propaganda?"

I handed them a Bible. They put it aside. They were not interested. They said, "No, we want to see what you teach. What do you teach?"

I had a handful of sermons in the back of my Bible and I said, "Here. This is what I teach." They looked at those for about thirty seconds and became totally bored. They weren't interested in my sermons and they kept pressing me, "What are you doing here? You are here illegally."

I said, "Sirs, here is my passport. Here are my papers. Here is my letter from the president's office that gives me the right to work in this place." They ignored them and said, "We know you are here illegally. What do you teach?"

This went on for an hour. My daughter Tamara later said, "Daddy, I know you were scared. I saw the sweat start under your arms and spread all the way to your belt loops." I was scared. I knew what these people did. They murdered, tortured, threw people in the *boot*—that's the trunk in American English—of the car. When they do, you usually are never heard of again.

Finally, in the midst of that interrogation, those men looked at me and said again, "What do you teach?"

Brothers and sisters, the power of God came upon me and I said to them, "I teach that all men have sinned, that God loves all men. Those who will repent can be saved and that's what you need to do right now in my house."

They looked at me. I pressed. They got very uneasy. Finally they stood up and said, "Listen, I think this man's okay. We had better leave now." As they started to leave, I said, "No, you can't leave yet. You are a guest in my house." (Well, I used that term a little bit loosely to say the least.) I said, "I always pray with my guests." I prayed with all my heart that God would break their hearts and that they would come to know Jesus as Savior.

When I got through, three of them dashed out the door. The fourth remained behind with tears in his eyes, trying to talk to me. I tried to talk to him until finally he hurried out of the house.

That was on Sunday. On Tuesday they got into a drunken brawl and one of these men was killed. They came to harass me but I belonged to God and God let them come because He wanted them to hear the Good News of Jesus Christ.

Three of my friends were arrested that day and all three of them were murdered, one of them decapitated. Those were the kinds of times we had during the Amin years but during that time some wonderful things happened. Cha Cha Said was a Muslim, an Asian Muslim about seventeen years old. Through a process of witnessing over a year, Cha Cha came to know Jesus as his Savior. His father was angry. One night his father brought him to my house in the middle of the night and said, "Take him . . . he's yours. I don't want him. I'm sorry for the day my wife ever bore him." He left him at my house and Cha Cha cried all night.

Finally, just three years ago, fourteen years later, my wife and I were asked to go to London to be Cha's Cha's father and mother at his wedding and to preach at it. We did. Today, almost sixteen years since he was saved, Cha Cha has two children. In London I have two grandchildren.

Jesus, the Author and Finisher of our faith. He is our Protector and I think of all that has happened in these years and I challenge others to look to Jesus, the Author and the Finisher of our faith.

In 1979, it became necessary for us to leave Uganda. We moved to Kenya. But I regularly crossed the border into Uganda and continued ministry there. Then we were able to return to Uganda just as soon as the war ended. We had many troubles. We were in the midst of relief efforts. A lot of relief food was stolen or misused. A lot of pastors had backslidden, and church money was being misused. Church pastors were involved in immorality and I became discouraged, but I kept preaching and ministering. My heart was broken and I was in a backslidden condition myself. I was not full of the power of God like I needed to be.

During that time, we were fishing for bass in Kenya at Lake Naivasha. Lake Naivasha is near where our children attend boarding school. My wife and our friend, Jerry Pearcy, had crossed the seven or eight miles across the lake and there caught forty-three bass in about two hours. Man, that was great! We love to fish and here we came back across the lake and got caught in a terrible rainstorm. Our boat sunk and we were in water that would kill you overnight through hypothermia. We were far from the shore, I think about two or three miles, and there we began to struggle for our lives at 6:15 PM.

I carried Doris on my back for an hour. I had a good life jacket; hers was not so good. Jerry Pearcy went into cold shock at about 10 PM. I grabbed him, took my belt, ran it through his belt loops, and tied it to the handle of a gas can. Then I tied it to my belt as I tried to make it to shore. I swam and swam. At that time I was running thirty miles a week and I was a strong swimmer but I couldn't make it to shore pulling both Doris and Jerry. The wind took us in four gigantic circles and we could not make it to shore.

Hour after hour passed and, when I saw the search lights disappear, I thought no boats were still searching. We had done a lot of praying. Shortly after midnight, my wife began to pray and she said, "Oh, God, we cannot save ourselves."

I believe that is where we are as Southern Baptists today. Southern Baptists are not God's last hope. God is *our* last hope. I stood there in the water and Doris said, "I rebuke you, Satan, in the Name of Jesus Christ. I know that you want to kill us, but we belong to God."

I said, "Yes. Yes."

Doris said, "Oh, Lord, we are helpless to save ourselves. If we are saved, You must save us."

That's the story of our lives. We cried out in agreement to God and then I cried out as I was doing every fifteen minutes, "Help." Unknown to me, about two miles over on the shore there was one boat still searching for us. They had sheared a pin in their propeller and they were up on the shore, looking for a nail to put into that hole. They found it and they heard me. At 12:30 AM I cried, "Help" again. They were right on top of us and we were rescued.

I'm here to tell you I learned something from that experience. I was grumbling, I was complaining, I was unhappy. I thought that surely I was in the wrong place and I cried to God in all of that. I thought, "Maybe God doesn't hear me anymore." But God did hear us and God showed me that day that He was able to deliver us. He Who delivered Daniel, Shadrach, Meshach, and Abednego is the God who delivered Harry and Doris—the God who can deliver you today. Our God is able to deliver us. Let us be in His Will.

The Lord's hand is not so short that it cannot save. Right now you may be in a sea of despair and your heart may be crying. Let me tell you—run the race. Let me beg you in the Name of Jesus, walk in the Spirit. Let me cry out unto you, be filled with the Spirit. Bring men and women to the Savior. We have need of preachers all over the world. If you are in God's Will here, praise God. But God wants some of you in Africa, Russia, or South America. God is saying to you, "Would you go?" You ought to say, "Yes, Lord, for I know that the safest place on the earth is the Will of God for me."

Then as I close, one of the great joys of my life occurred in 1984. We had seen forty-five churches that started and stayed. We had started about twenty-five that didn't stay but we had about forty-five churches that had stayed and sixty pastors into whom we had poured 650 hours of Bible training and discipleship. We were thrilled about that but we had worshipped off and on in our house for years. We had been unable to get a town church because Baptists are not looked up to. Catholics and Angelicans are, but not Baptists.

But we had prayed, "Oh, God, we want a church. Give us three couples to disciple." Starting in January, 1984, God gave us William and Grace Eyika. I baptized them. I taught them how to have a quiet time, pray, and study their Bible. I taught them the doctrine of God, Christ, the Holy Spirit, sin, Satan, baptism, the Lord's Supper, the Judgment, and the second coming of the Lord Jesus Christ. We discipled them and they began discipling others. My wife taught them how to teach Sunday School.

God gave us a second couple, Henry and Grace Hamala. I was discipling Grace who was already a Christian. Her husband came under a tree in my front yard. I said to Henry, "The Bible says in 1 John 5:12, 'He who has the Son has the life. He who does not have the Son does not have the life.' Do you have the Son?" He said, "I do not." I showed him how and he was saved under that tree. Oh, how he loved the Lord and His church!

Then came Ben and Mary Ariko. Three couples—we discipled them all. In a few months we were running seventy to eighty-five in our front living room. God used my preacher brother, Fred Garvin, a home missionary in Winfield, Kansas, to bring a team of builders to Uganda from Kansas and we built a beautiful brick building. We finished that building. Well, just two weeks before we came home in August of 1985, God gave us that church. Although our house in Uganda was destroyed on February fourth of this year [1986], the church is still there. All my notes, library, and language translation work we had done were destroyed, but the church is still there. The house was left a shell by the fleeing army that was displaced when a new government came in during January. But the church is still there.

I got a letter just this past month and they said, "We are doing well in the church. We have twenty-two people who recently came to the Lord Jesus and we have about thirteen ready to be baptized." Praise God. I've seen over seven thousand people baptized in the last sixteen years. I've had over a hundred one-on-one disciples and I praise God for it. I don't do it in Uganda only, I do it in the states for whether it's here or there, if God is in it, we can reach the world with the gospel. You are important and I am important. We are God's plan for reaching the world for the Lord Jesus Christ.

Would you please, this week, consider God's Perfect Will for your life as I do for mine. "Father, oh, Father God, break our hearts. Give us compassion for the lost and flood us with love for the black, the white, the brown, or any other beautiful color that God makes people. Bless our churches, our Convention with revival, with spiritual renewal, with a holy hatred of sin, and with a hunger for the fullness of the Holy Spirit. Bless us with a desire to see men and women saved and to plant churches in our country and around the world. In Jesus' Name I pray."

7

The Atonement: Man's Need for Christ's Provision

by Bill Tolar

Bill Tolar

W. B. Tolar, native of Jonesboro, Louisiana, has served as dean
of the School of Theology, Southwestern Baptist Theological
Seminary, Fort Worth, Texas, since 1981. Formerly, he was
professor of biblical backgrounds there since 1965. Between
1950 and 1956 he was pastor of three churches in Texas. He
holds B.A. and M.A. degrees from Baylor University and the
M.Div. and Th.D. degrees from Southwestern Seminary. He
has studied and lectured in forty-eight countries on four conti-
nents, including twenty-eight times in Israel. He is married to
the former Floye Kimball. They have two children, William
and Lora Mae.

7

The Atonement: Man's Need for Christ's Provision

by Bill Tolar

In the year AD 68, a young Roman Emperor by the name of Claudius Drusus Lucius Domitius Ahenobarbus (better known as Nero) came to a moment of crisis in his life. An army was marching on Rome from Spain under the leadership of a general named Galba. Nero, in that moment, realized he could not defend himself. So as General Galba came, Nero, not yet thirty-one, ordered a slave to hold a dagger and, in the midst of that, the slave helped him to take his own life.

Galba became emperor and lasted only until another Roman general by the name of Otho got there. He lasted only until a third general by the name of Vitellius got there. He lasted only until a fourth general by the name of Vespasian got there. I think it was in the midst of that turmoil of AD 68-69 that God may have inspired the writer of the book from whom the previous preachers have used their text and from which I draw my text.

Go with me to Hebrews 10. I think very likely it was in the persecution of Christians in the tumult of the blaming of those Christians for the burning of Rome by Nero in 64 that caused the author, under the leadership of the Holy Spirit, to write words of encouragement to Christians facing difficult times. I believe there is a message for us on the Atonement in the midst of that.

Many of you studied and taught the book of Hebrews this past January or February [1986] in the January Bible Study. You will remember that the inspired writer, writing to perhaps Jewish Christians primarily, so they'd not be discouraged by the awesome difficulty of their day, wrote in a brilliant series of at last seven ways Jesus Christ is infinitely superior to any and everything that had ever come before, and that would ever come after it. Christ is superior, he said, to the prophets. He is superior to the angels. He is superior to Moses. He is superior to the High Priests. He was a superior sacrifice, serves under a superior covenant, and offers the greatest eternal sacrifice and in that sacrifice He deals with the Atonement and in Hebrews 9, verse 22 that I want to read for the main text, the writer says in the closing words "and without the shedding of blood is no remission." The NASB states it, "without the shedding of blood there is no forgiveness."

But my main text is Hebrews 10:10-14.

By the which will we are sanctified through the offering of the body of Jesus Christ once for all. And every priest standeth daily ministering and offering oftentimes and the same sacrifices, which can never take away sins: But this man, after he had offered one sacrifice for sins for ever, sat down on the right hand of God; From henceforth expecting till his enemies be made his footstool. For by one offering he hath perfected for ever them that are sanctified.

The key text and the key verse is verse 12: "For this man," a reference to the God-man, Jesus Christ, "after he had offered one sacrifice for sins forever, sat down on the right hand of God." In that verse are two key ideas I want to build my message around. He said, "One sacrifice Christ offered for sins for ever." Let's look first of all at the reason or the necessity of the Atonement—human sin. He offered His sacrifice for sin. So let's look first of all at mankind's need of Atonement. Then we will look at the first part of the verse, Christ's offering. His sacrifice, and that will be Christ's gracious provision for mankind.

But first of all, mankind's need for Atonement. Modern Americans, sophisticated and educated, and the world in general do not share and accept our biblical view of human sinfulness and the critical spiritual condition we are in when we are lost. So as we look at human need, let's notice first the unbeliever's view of his condition, the secularist's view of his condition, the lost person's opinion of himself, and the viewpoint we ourselves had before we came to know Christ as Lord and Savior.

If I could put you in a time machine of some kind (like there used to be in the newspaper comic strip "Alley Oop"), set the dial to 1900-1905-1910-1913, and let you hear what some leading politicians and others were saying then about the innate basic goodness of mankind, you'd almost shake your head in unbelief because they were being influenced profoundly by Darwin's theory of evolution. Many of them were saying as the twentieth century began that, since persons had evolved biologically, mankind would now evolve spiritually and morally. Many of them were saying that persons were not sinners as preachers of the Bible were saying, they were not depraved as theologians said, but that we are basically sweet, gentle, and good. The reason why we fought and killed was because we were hungry, ill-housed, or ill-clothed, and many of them said,

"All you've got to do is educate mankind better, give us better circumstances and we will virtually bring in a utopia."

It was the day of almost inevitable progress on the part and belief of many people in the innate goodness of mankind. In the midst of that, World War I broke out. But you see, one of the things they had said in 1905 and 1910 on that almost inevitable progress was that the twentieth century would be the century of no wars. They said that if we would get an education, better housing, and better food, we'd lay aside wars like a child outgrows a toy. But Germany which began World War I was not a nation of illiterates, not a nation of poverty. The very two things learned persons said caused war were not evident in widespread proportions in the German nation.

A nation and a century of no wars, they said. Therefore, it shattered the foundations of some of the beliefs in inevitable goodness of mankind. The secularist says mankind does not need God, that God is the product of human imagination. The secularist says we can do it by ourselves. But if man can do it by himself, then Nero should have done it when he was emperor. He became emperor when he was only sixteen years old. He would rule fourteen years. You and I know him best for the burning of Rome, but listen to what historians said of Nero as a sixteen- and seventeen-year-old emperor. Contemporary Roman historians said, "He is affable. He is generous. He is gracious. He is intelligent. The future is bright because this flower of Roman civilization will lead us on to the heights of human aspiration."

In fourteen years power corrupted the young emperor. The old adage is that, "Power corrupts and absolute power corrupts absolutely." In fourteen years look at what Nero, a man come of age, did without God. During those fourteen years he ordered his own mother to be murdered—assassinated because she tried to correct his runaway deprivation. He stomped and kicked to death his own wife, who was carrying his child at the time. He stomped her and kicked her until she died in agony. He ordered Seneca, the brilliant philosopher, to commit suicide because his professor had tried to correct his runaway passion and increasingly degradated life-style. He became so depraved he had handsome young men tied at stakes, stripped of their clothes, and beautiful young women stripped of their clothes, tied at the stake. Then he got down on all fours and ordered a tiger-, leopard-, or lion skin draped over his body. Walking on all fours, he would attack them with his fingernails and teeth, biting them all over. Now at the age of thirty-one, he would order a slave to hold a dagger and take his own life. If man, without God, if man, with power, if man only with education, if man with only his own efforts, if man alone can do it, then Nero should have done it but he ended his life in tragedy and in sorrow.

When I was a college teacher many years ago, I lived in a city in Texas where there was an air force base. It was later closed by as an economy move of the national budget, but in those days it was open. One afternoon a young air force officer got off work, came into the city there where we lived, picked up his estranged wife who was pregnant with his fifth child, got their four children, all under the age of ten, and drove to the west side of that city where there was a lake into which some rivers flowed. They got into a violent argument because the young man—who had four children and another one coming—had been seeing other women and the wife did not like it. The argument became violent. Unknown to her, he got out of the car, the paper said, did something to the tubing that carried the fluid to his brakes, knowing that the next time he pumped his brakes they would fail. He got back into the car without telling his wife what had happened.

Instead of going over an old bridge to a playground area on the river, he turned off the main road and headed toward the river where there was a straight drop of nearly ten feet to the water level. He pumped his brakes as he got near the edge of the water. He pumped his brakes and, as he got near the edge of the river, there were no brakes. That car with those six people plunged off the bank and sank immediately.

Not too far away a group of young people heard the splash and turned to see. They did not see who was in the car when it hit the water, but they saw one head come up out of the water. As they started toward it, they saw only the young husband and father come up. They saw another head, the head of the wife come up. They saw him put his hand on his expectant wife's head and push her under the water until he saw them coming. Not until then did he turn loose. They heard her screaming frantically but they could not understand her until they got close and discovered she was screaming about her children being in the car.

One of those college young people lived only two blocks from me. He was among the first to get to the car. He said, "Dr. Tolar, when we learned there were children in the car, we dove down to the car. The mud from the bottom of the river was so thick we could not see inside. The car had come down on the nose, apparently there was water trapped in the top. Apparently the children were able to get into that bubble but for some reason the water pressure had closed the door or the mud had closed it and they could not get it open. They pulled and tugged and knocked and jerked but to no avail. They could not get the doors open out of which the parents had apparently come. The young student said, "I cupped my ear to the car. I could hear the screams and shrieks of the children with their heads in the air bubble inside. I tore at the glass, I knocked and pushed and all the flesh was torn from my knuckles. Suddenly I realized the bubbles had ceased, the screams had stopped. I realized that only inches from me the children had drowned. All four children under the age of ten drowned in that car while their father sat only twenty feet away on the bank without turning a hand to help them at all."

That college boy looked into my eyes and asked me a question I have never forgotten, a question that I ask this Pastors' Conference and those of you who are here. He asked me, "Dr. Tolar, what's wrong with human nature? What is wrong with human nature? What is wrong with the human race? It's not just this incident but the daily papers report robbery, rape, killing, wars, fighting. Dr. Tolar, what is wrong with the human race?"

The Bible says sin has come, twisted, warped, and made necessary an atonement. We must have something done for us we cannot do for ourselves. The Bible's view of man's condition is radically different from that of the secularist, unbelieving, natural person. For instance, in Isaiah 59, Isaiah said of his people that they had bloody hands (v. 3). Did Isaiah mean that everybody in his day was a physical murderer? No. But in Matthew 5, Jesus says if we are angry without just cause, that's as serious as the Old Testament command not to murder. I'd like to meet that human being who has never been noble even once without just cause, who has never been angry out of envy, out of jealousy, out of resentment. Which of us this morning, where is that person in the world who does not fall under Isaiah's description? We stand before the righteous God with bloody hands. We are guilty of it. 1 John 3:15 says, "Whosoever hateth his brother is a murderer and ye know that no murderer hath eternal life abiding in him." Isaiah said of his day, "they have lying tongues."

Bring me that human being, however civil, however nice, however gracious, however generous, that has never one time so changed facts as to mislead, that has not mixed some error in with truth, that has not deceived and misled and therefore would have to say there has come at some time a falsehood or lie. But if we have, we have broken one of the commandments. The ninth commandment not to bear false witness means not to tell an untruth, not to tell a lie and James 2:10 says, ". . . whosoever shall keep the whole law, and yet offend in one point, he is guilty of all." We are as guilty as if we have broken all the commandments of God.

Let me illustrate it like this. It's like being in a container attached to the bottom of a helicopter by a hundred-foot-long chain. If the helicopter were three-thousand feet high, how many links in the chain would have to break to send us falling to our death? All the links? Of course not. Only one. One sin against an Infinite God equals an infinite sin. You and I need the atonement, someone, something to do something for us, for our hands are bloody, our tongues have lied.

Isaiah said also that people have wayward feet. If a tornado hit your city, looters would come with wayward feet to spoil your belongings. Some of them would be neighbors from your city, from your locality, not just outsiders. Feet that run to evil. Jeremiah said we have wicked hearts. He said the "heart is deceitful above all things, and desperately wicked . . ." (17:9). Which of us has never shared with Paul in Romans 7:19, "That which I would do not: that which I would not I find myself doing"? Bloody hands, lying tongues, wayward feet, wicked hearts. In Isaiah 59:7, the prophet said that their thoughts were only thoughts of evil. And in Revelation 21:8, when, in that great day of judgment, Satan shall be thrown into the lake of fire that burns forever, that horrendous list of sins does not begin with murderers and whoremongers, it begins with the fearful and unbelieving. Then follow the murderer, the whoremonger, and the unbelieving individuals.

How many times have I had a college student say to me, "Professor Tolar, I've got a friend who is not a Christian. He's such a good person but just doesn't believe in Jesus as Lord and Savior." Oh, the unbelieving minds—the greatest sin of all. The other sins can be pardoned and forgiven but the Bible says that over against the secularist, unbelieving, natural person's view, we have bloody hands, we have lying tongues, we have wayward feet, we have wicked hearts, we have unbelieving minds. Draw a line. The sum total is: we are lost in sin, we are doomed to an eternity without God. We need someone, something to help us in the midst of our desperation. Oh, dear God in heaven, do something for us for we cannot help ourselves!

When I was a college student, I roomed with an All-American football player. He was not only a great football player, he was a great basketball player, a great boxer, a great golfer. He was a physiological genius. I saw him do many things but one thing especially interested me that he did while working out for a Golden Gloves tournament. He was jumping rope and I asked him, "How about standing on your rope as you are working out?" He got each end of that rope in his hand and he said, "Yes." Then I asked that All-American physiological genius just to pick up 195 pounds himself. No way, no way. He wouldn't even try to pick himself up.

But there are people in America today, there are people in the world today who seem to think we can just pick ourselves up by our bootstraps. I tell you, it is just as spiritually impossible as it is physically impossible to lift ourselves up and say, "God, look how good and kind and sweet I am. All I need is a little change outwardly and I will be good enough for heaven." The Bible says we are in a crisis. Our need . . . mankind's desperate need is why the Bible says God sent His Son.

Paul said in Galatians 4:4, "In the fulness of time God sent forth His Son." The writer of Hebrews said, "And this man, Jesus, after he had offered one sacrifice for sins for all time, sat down at the right hand of God; From henceforth expecting till his enemies be made his footstool" (10:12).

In closing, let's look at Christ's gracious provision. Human need is dark, awesome, and critical. Human need is for atonement—something that will make us right before God. The word *atonement* means "something to satisfy"—reparation for an injury or wrong done, something offered that will satisfy the wronged person. How can we, wrong in our sin, make right with God? Can we do it? The Bible says no, but Christ has done it for us.

There are five things I want you to notice about what Christ has done—His provision for us. First of all, Christ's provision for atonement was foreshadowed in the sacrifices of the Old Testament. I challenge anybody to read the Book of Exodus about the Passover and then read the Gospels when Jesus instituted the Lord's Supper at the Passover feast. They took an unblemished male goat or sheep. They took it and sacrificed it without breaking of bone. They took blood and put it on either side and above the door. Draw a line from the blood over the door to the ground. You have a perfectly foreshadowed cross. Christ didn't have a bone broken when He died. The Roman soldiers broke the limbs of those malefactors on either side. There is a beautiful, mysterious foreshadowing of the sacrifice of Christ's atonement even in the Passover—His broken body and shed blood.

Read about the consecration of priests in Exodus 29 and then read in Hebrews the atonement that Christ makes for us. Read about the consecration of the altar of incense in Exodus 30 and then read about Christ making it possible for us to come into the presence of God in the Book of Hebrews. See how John the Baptist pointed out Jesus as the Lamb of God. Read Hebrews 13:11-12 where that inspired writer discussed the blood and bodies of animals offered in the temple, taken outside the gate and burned. He wrote, "Therefore Christ suffered outside the gate" (13:12). I think the atonement of Christ is foreshadowed throughout the Old Testament, especially in the sacrifices.

Second, it was predicted by the prophets. Read Isaiah 53. "He was wounded for our transgressions, he was bruised for our iniquities" (v. 5). Read Psalm 22. "They pierced my hands and feet, they sneered and laughed. They cast lots for my garments" (vv. 16, 18). There is an awesome, mysterious, marvelous portrayal predicted by the prophets that the One who would come would suffer for us. His atonement was foreshadowed in the sacrifices predicted by the prophets.

Third, it was willed by the Father. In Matthew 26 is the account of Jesus in the Garden of Gethsemane. He said, "Father, if it be possible, let this cup pass from me: nevertheless not as I will, but as thou wilt" (v. 39). In John 12, the Greeks came and Jesus said, "Father, save Me from this hour. But for this hour came I into the world. Glorify thyself, O Father" (vv. 27-28). God said, "I have glorified it, and will glorify it again." God would glorify Himself in the death of His Son. Willed by the Father. Intended, purposed by God the Father that His Son die for us. Hebrews 5:7 says Jesus learned obedience by what

He suffered. In 1 Peter 3:17-18 the Bible says, "If it be the will of God that you suffer," (author's paraphrase). The Scripture implies that it was the will of God that Christ die for us. Christ's gracious atonement, His gracious provision, foreshadowed in the sacrifices, predicted by the prophets, willed by the Father, but accomplished by the Son.

All of that led up to that awesome day when Jesus Christ died on the cross and did something to satisfy all the demands of the righteous God. He did something so awesome it would wash, cleanse, and purify all the sins that you and I might have. It was accomplished by the Son of God who gave Himself. Jesus said in Matthew 20, "Even as the Son of man came not to be ministered unto, but to minister, and to give his life a ransom for many" (v. 28). He came for that purpose. He gave Himself. He said, "No man taketh my life from me, I give it." Christ lay down His life. The atonement was made by the Son lovingly, unbelievingly, overwhelmingly, eternally for us.

Then last, it was witnessed to by the Holy Spirit. If it was willed by the Father and done by the Son, how does something that was done two thousand years ago come to transform ple that you've heard give their testimonies? How can a fallen person have their lives radically transformed? How can a life be so twisted and yet be made so straight? It is the power and work of the Holy Spirit for in John 16:8-9 Jesus, speaking about the coming Comforter, the Spirit, said, "He will convict you of sin, and righteousness, and judgment" (author's paraphrase). He will convict the world of sin because, "they believe not in Me." Miracle of miracles, wonder of wonders, what Jesus Christ did two thousand years ago can be taken by the Holy Spirit, applied to our lives and make us dead in sin, alive forever more. In our darkness His light can come and transform us. Bound for hell, He can turn us to heaven, can remake us. Alienated from God, He can make us right with Him. Lovers of self, He can make us lovers of the Savior. The Spirit of God must take the atonement of Christ and apply it to our lives.

In 1 Corinthians 12:3, Paul said, "No man can say of Jesus, 'He is Lord' except by the Spirit of God" (author's paraphrase). Therefore the atonement of Christ, foreshadowed in the sacrifice, predicted by the prophets, willed by the Father, done by the Son, is witnessed to by the Holy Spirit in our lives to the glory and honor of God Himself.

As I close my message, let me say I am a testimony to the work of the Spirit of God, using the written Word of God. I was born into a family that never went to church. I never saw my mother and father in church or in Sunday School. I saw my mother's body one time when her casket was brought into a church for her funeral. I never sat one time beside a mother and father to sing the praises of the church and to know the presence of God's people. I never saw my father in the church until my conversion and my surrender to the Christian ministry. Then he came to hear his youngest son preach.

I was a freshman in high school, heard a high school phys-ed teacher say to a group of boys, "Boys, I want to challenge you to do something that 99 percent of the people of the world cannot say they've done and that includes college graduates." "What is that?" we asked? She said, "To read the world's best-seller completely through, line for line, word for word." And we said, "What is the world's best-seller?" She held the book up and said, "It is the Bible. If you will read three chapters a day Monday through Saturday, five on Sunday, then one year from today you can say you've done something that 99 percent of the people of the world cannot say they have done."

I regret to say it was not out of religious interest for I had never gone to church in my life but I wanted to say I had read the world's best-seller and I started the journey through. After I delivered my papers early each morning, I sat out on the front porch of my home in North Central Louisiana and started my journey. I began to notice after a few weeks reading that it was only at that time of day I sensed an awesome presence that began to be there. After a while that presence became so real and so awesome, (I did not see visions, I heard no voices,) but I sensed something so real and powerful as the presence and reality of anything in this room today. I realized if I were going to continue to live my selfish, self-centered ways, I had to close the book and put it out or I'd be compelled by conscience and intelligence to give my heart and life to the God Who spoke there.

I stand before you today because the Holy Spirit of God took what Jesus Christ did two thousand years ago and into my emptiness He brought a fullness, into my darkness He brought a light, into my ignorant hatred He brought a love and my life was transformed because the Spirit of God took the atoning blood of Jesus and applied it to me and my life changed forevermore. Praise God. I shall sing His praises throughout eternity because what He did in the midst of my need was to give His Son to meet my eternal need. Human need and Christ's precious provision. Thank God for the incredible gift that atones for us and makes us right with a living God.

8
The Secret of Ultimate Living

By Bailey Smith

Bailey Smith

Bailey Smith, a native Texan, is a Southern Baptist evangelist. Formerly, he was pastor of First Southern Baptist Church, Del City, Oklahoma (1973-85); First Baptist Church, Warren, Arkansas, and First Baptist Church, Hobbs, New Mexico. He holds the B.A. degree from Ouachita Baptist University, Arkadelphia, Arkansas, and the B.D. degree from Southwestern Baptist Theological Seminary, Fort Worth, Texas. In 1979 he served as president of the Baptist General Convention of Oklahoma and as president of the Southern Baptist Convention, 1980-81. He has also served as president of the SBC Pastors' Conference. He is married to the former Sandra Elliff. They have three sons: Scott, Steve, and Josh.

8
The Secret of Ultimate Living

by Bailey Smith

An old man and woman getting on a train were almost run over by a young whippersnapper. He just knocked the old lady down, knocked the luggage out of their hands, and they were battered and bruised by this crass young man trying to get ahead of them on them on the train. Well, as fate would have it, when they did get on the train they discovered they were seated right across from that young man who was seated beside a beautiful girl. The old man was especially angry because of how that fellow had treated his wife by running into them, knocking them over, and he couldn't believe they were seated right across from the one who had treated them so rudely.

As they were traveling the young man was flirting with the beautiful girl seated beside him. He was very rude, very forward, very aggressive. After a few miles of travel they went through a dark tunnel and all of a sudden you heard the sound of a kiss. There was a kiss and then a slap. When they got on the other side of the tunnel, the young girl was thinking, "Ahuh, that old man tried to get fresh with his wife and she slapped him." The old woman was thinking, "Yeah, that young fellow tried to kiss that beautiful girl while we were in the tunnel and she slapped his face." The young man was thinking while rubbing his face, "You know, this girl had that old man lean across and try to kiss her. She thought it was me and she slapped me." But the old man, with a grin of satisfaction on his face, was thinking, "I've never had so much fun in my life. I kissed the back of my hand and slapped the fool out of that young fellow."

Not everything appears to be what it is. The Cross appeared to be defeat but it was victory. The Cross appeared to be the end, but it was the beginning. The Cross appeared to be the wrong way to get people to heaven, but it was the right way. I'm convinced that the message is still the blood-stained Cross. Persons can still be redeemed. Persons can still be changed and I have an optimistic, encouraging word for you today. Not only can Christ give us heaven by dying on the Cross, but He can get heaven inside us. What a glorious truth to know that you can have heaven on the way to heaven.

I was reading an advertisement for an expensive, foreign car. It said that the car is the ultimate driving machine. I saw a tour company advertisement in my hotel room and it says that the company's cruise to the Bahamas is the ultimate vacation. Others say the ultimate cruise is to go to the Virgin Islands. Wherever we turn there is that word *ultimate*. I tell you that if we can ever learn the ultimate way of living, life for us would be so joyous, so victorious.

Every place I turn as I have preached in forty-seven states, I find discouraged pastors. I mean they are discouraged. Men so low they could skip rope under the bed and never bump their head on the slats. They are low, discouraged, and down. But if you know Jesus, you have found life's greatest answer. Pastors, staff members, wives, I want to tell you that I've got a good word for you. I want to give you the formula that even as a pastor, even during your struggles, you can live to its ultimate extent.

So many people are worried. So many people are getting bad news. A doctor called a man and said to that man, "I have gotten your tests back and I have read the results of your physical examination." The doctor then said to the man, "I've got some bad news and some good news. What do you want first?" The man said, "Well, doctor, I want the good news first." The doctor said, "Well, the good news is that you have two days to live." The man replied, "That's the good news? What's the bad news?" The doctor said, "I tried to call you yesterday."

Ladies and gentlemen, I've got only good news for you. And the word came from what Jesus said while on the Cross. It's in the Book of Luke, chapter 23, verses 46 and 47,

> And when Jesus had cried with a loud voice, he said, Father, into thy hands I commend my spirit: and having said thus, he gave up the ghost. Now when the centurion saw what was done, he glorified God, saying, Certainly this was a righteous man.

Here we discover the secret of ultimate living. *Father* is the ultimate relationship. *Into thy hands,* is the ultimate security. *Commit* is the ultimate commitment. *My spirit* is the ultimate success. Let's look at them one by one. First of all in the secret of ultimate living, Jesus taught us the ultimate relationship. What is the ultimate relationship of life? It's to know God as the Father. The very first recorded words out of the mouth of Jesus were, "I must be about my Father's business." In the Sermon on the Mount, Jesus said the word *Father* seventeen times. In the gospel of John, the word *Father* is used forty-two times. And even when you go to that great prayer called the High

Priestly Prayer of Jesus in John 17, you see where Jesus again uses the word *Father* six times.

I have been to many seminars on "How To Get Along With Your Wife" or "How To Get Along With Your Husband," "How To Get Along With Your Parents," "How To Get Along With Your Children." Ladies and gentlemen, I tell you if you ever learn that God is your Father, your Heavenly Father, that is the ultimate relationship. That puts all other relationships into the right perspective. I am so glad that my God is not an obese Buddha with a sunken navel in granite. I'm so glad that my God is a Holy God, He is my Father. I'm so glad that my God is not one of the thousand gods of Hinduism, but my God is a Father. Our God is the One God, the Jehovah God, not disassociated from us in the heavens but I can look upon my God and say as Jesus did as an example from the Cross, "Father." That is the ultimate relationship.

I'm so grateful I have a Father in heaven. Do you know that Jesus made it so clear that He is the begotten of the Father. You say, "Well, Bailey, don't you believe that we are as much the sons of God as Jesus?" Not really. While He is our Father, He is begotten. Jesus is different. The word *begotten* means literally "Out of the loins of God the Father came forth Jesus." So-and-so begat so-and-so, so-and-so begat so-and-so, and begat, and begat, and begat. That means they were literally the father. They sired their offspring. In the sense that God's blood literally flowed in the veins of Jesus Christ as His own personal geneological Son, He is different. Not only that, but when you and I refer to God as the Father, we are the only ones who can do it. I still believe Jesus was correct when He said, "I'm the way, the truth and the life and no man comes to the Father but by me." Only Christians can call God "Father." He is the Father in heaven.

A lady said to me in Florida, "I don't like that narrow-minded view." I said, "You don't get a vote." It doesn't matter what you think. It matters what God says. That settles the issue. I want to tell you if a television talk show came on and they asked about the veracity of the Word of God. If everybody in the studio and everybody who called in said, "No, the Bible isn't true," the Bible would still be the infallible, inerrant Word of God. I remember reading recently again the story of the Prodigal Son. The son comes home, a ring on his finger, shoes on his feet. What a wonderful success. The fatted calf is killed but I notice the one thing the father never did. As much as he was a father, there is one thing the father never did to get his boy home—he never went to the hog pen.

There are people who say, "The Bible says this, preacher say that. If only the church would compromise." Ladies and gentlemen, I would like to tell you God will not cater to the idiosyncrasies of anybody. God will not get in the hog pen of silly religious ideas. A man or woman will come in faith and repentance, believing Jesus is the only way to heaven or they will not get there. There is no other way.

I'm so glad that God is our Father. When I was fourteen years old I worked at a breakfast shop in Colorado Springs, Colorado. I remember one night a Colorado blizzard came. I stepped out into the alley and looked as the snow was blowing parallel to the earth. I looked up into the streetlights and I could see in the contrast of the snow and the light how thick the snow was. It was bitter cold. It was six miles to where I lived in Manitou Springs and I rode my bicycle every night after midnight the six miles to my home, whatever the weather might be. I wondered how I would make it home that night.

I closed up. I mopped the floor, went out the back door, put my coat up around my neck, pulled a scarf around it tightly, and was ready to get on my bicycle. Just as I was pulling my bicycle out into the street, our old 1954 Ford drove up and my Dad was behind the wheel. I could see that exhaust coming out of that tail pipe. My Dad got out of the car and said, "Son, I looked outside and saw how bad it was and I thought you could just take that old bicycle and put it in the back of this car and we'd drive home together." Folks, when I got in that warm car, I tell you, I was so grateful to be warm and by the side of my father. What a wonderful time it was going home.

What I'm telling you, discouraged pastor, what I'm telling you, dear friend, is that our God has identified with our sins. He has identified with our sins, He has identified with our needs, He has come in the form of a Servant, obedient unto death, even the death of the Cross. God has highly exalted Him, given Him a Name that is above every other Name, that at the Name of Jesus every knee shall bow and every tongue shall confess Jesus Christ. I want to tell you something, when you feel all alone, don't you do it. The Father is very near, helping you, identifying with you, strengthening you.

Second, let me say not only is the secret to ultimate living the ultimate relationship of Father, but Jesus also said, "Into *thy hands* I commend my spirit." That is the ultimate security. I believe that if I were an artist I, out of memory, could paint the hands of my mother. I remember her hands even though she died at forty-one years of age. I still believe I could paint her hands if I had that ability. I remember when my father was killed as a pastor trying to build a new church in Dallas. They placed his hands in that casket, across his chest, and I still remember looking at those strong hands that had held me, worked for me, and labored in my behalf. I also remember, frankly, those hands getting my attention, but I was thankful for the strong hands of my father. Secure. We have been disappointed of late learning that NASA is not secure. The military is not secure. Three of our missiles have blown up. Three in a row have exploded in our face. Our technology is not secure.

But I turn to John, chapter 10, verse 29 and I read that "My Father is greater than all and he has me in his hands and all the power of heaven nor hell nor earth can pry open the hands of God." But I want to know all of us are secure in God's hands. It's no wonder that Jesus said, "Into thy hands I commit my spirit." I tell you folks, I got on shouting ground the other day. I said, "God, let me be a charismatic for five minutes." I began to read where when we get to heaven God is going to wipe away all the tears from our eyes. I first thought, what are the sources of those tears? I believe the source of tears in heaven is twofold. I believe, number one, some of us will weep when we get to heaven and we see we don't get the cloud we wanted and we didn't labor enough on behalf of Jesus. I believe some of us will weep when we step inside the Gates of Pearl because we will see heaven is more than we ever thought; Jesus is more glorious than we ever imagined; the streets of gold are more precious than we ever dreamed. We'll see all the saints that have come and we are going to say, "Oh, God, why didn't I preach harder? Why didn't I labor more? Why didn't I do more? Why didn't I work for you?" And all of a sudden the hand of God will come and take His hand and wipe the tears from our eyes.

I've got some good friends who if I'm in sorrow, will put a hand on my shoulder. I've got some good friends that if I'm in sorrow will even come up and embrace me. I have friends that if I'm in need they will write me a note of sympathy, encouragement, and condolence. But I don't know many people in my life who would come up to my face and take their hands and wipe away my tears. But when you and I stand before God, no tears will remain because with those secure, powerful hands He'll wipe away the tears from our eyes. What a great and glorious God!

I was reading the other day something that blessed me so much. Do you know how great this universe is? It is so mammoth that if you were to travel the speed of light 186,000 miles per second, in two seconds you would be past the moon. In eight minutes you would be past the sun. In five months you would be to the edge of our solar system. In four years you would come to our nearest star. Now did you hear me? In four years traveling 186,000 miles per second, you would finally come to the nearest star. Then if you decided to get out of our Milky Way, which is our galaxy, you would travel one-hundred thousand years at 186,000 miles per second to do so and if you wanted to go to the nearest galaxy, you would travel a million-and-a-half years at 186,000 miles per second to get to our nearest galaxy and now we know there are literally millions of galaxies. We now have telescopes that can see four-and-a-half billion light-years into space. Yet I pick up the Word of God and read Isaiah 40:12 where it says that our God even has the oceans in the palm of His hand—that same God who is so big, so strong, so powerful, as mammoth as our universe is, is so great that you can put every ocean of the world in the palm of His hand. It is that God who holds onto you. Thank God for His glorious truth.

The ultimate security. Third, He offers not only the ultimate relationship—*Father*—the ultimate security—*into thy hands*—but also the ultimate commitment. Jesus gave us the example of *Father,*—the ultimate relationship, *into thy hands,*—the ultimate security. But He also said, *I commit.* That Greek word *paratithemai* literally means "I deliver." Jesus said to Pilate, "Pilate, you have no power that my Heavenly Father does not give you." Jesus had just said to Herod, "No man takes my life from me." I've always been offended when I sing a song that says, "And Jesus spilled His blood." My friend, Jesus never spilled a drop of His blood. The word *spilled* means "accidental pouring." But Jesus poured it out freely that I might be saved, to cover my sins that I might be born again.

Southern Baptists, do you realize what could happen if you and I had the commitment Jesus had to say, "Lord, my soul, my body, my spirit, I *(paratithemai)* literally take it from myself and I deliver it into Your hands, I belong to You." That's why Jesus said about the Cross in Luke 14 that "a man who does not pick up his cross and follow Me is not worthy of Me." We've got to be willing to give our life.

I've had people say, "Well, you know, I've got financial stresses, I'm bearing my cross." That's not a cross. They say, "Well, I've been going through all kinds of difficulty, we've had sickness, I'm really bearing my cross." That's not a cross. I've had people say, "Well, my mother-in-law has moved in with us. I'm bearing my cross." Well, that may be a cross. But you know what Jesus meant.

I think Billy Graham is right when he says, "Had Jesus said that today, He would never have said 'cross.'" I want you to ponder that. Do you realize that had Jesus spoken Luke, chapter 14 in this generation, He would have never used the phrase, "You must bear your cross." Jesus would have said, "If you are going to follow me, you must be able to pick up your electric chair." The cross was the place of execution. Can't you just imagine churches and cathedrals with electric chairs on top instead of crosses? But Jesus said, "If you follow Me, you must be willing to take up your cross. You must be willing to take up an instrument of electrocution, an instrument of execution, and be willing to die for Me."

We need a new commitment to evangelism. Last year we baptized two thousand people fewer per week than we did the week before. I recently preached a crusade in a city that in the last twenty years has increased by ten-thousand population. I'm talking about a city in Texas. It's increased by ten thousand but the Southern Baptist Sunday School attendance has decreased by a thousand. I tell you folks, there is only one thing I know that Jesus died for and that's people. We need to get about the people business, loving people, sharing our faith, letting them know that some other denomination does not have a monopoly on the Holy Spirit. Southern Baptists still stand for moral issues.

I was standing to speak at the Arkansas state evangelism conference. Just as I stood to speak, the director in Arkansas said, "Bailey, just a minute." I did not go to the platform, he came to the platform and announced about the shuttle explosion and all of us dropped our heads and we prayed for the families and for our nation. "What a tragedy," we said. Seven precious Americans gone. We all wept, we were all sorry, we all empathized. The president attended some of the funerals, he payed homage to the families. But ladies and gentlemen, on the same day that seven American astronauts died, four-thousand babies were murdered by abortion in America and nobody wept. It's time somebody weeps.

Not long ago a lady in New York City took a Tylenol tablet, reportedly so, and died. We are all sorry for that but while one lady died and they took Tylenol off the shelf in that form, last year a quarter-of-a-million Americans died because of alcohol-related accidents. I believe it is time somebody said that alcohol is the insanity of this generation. God help us to do so.

Oh, let's get a commitment and bring people again to the foot of the cross. Southern Baptists, we can win this world. We've got a battle but we cannot win this world, we cannot preach with power, we cannot preach as they did on Pentecost Day and so many people came to know Jesus. We cannot be the powerful Baptists we've always been. We cannot be the Southern Baptists that God has anointed and blessed if we put question marks over the authority, power, and truthfulness of God's Word. We cannot do it. Some have even said we can get to God through prayers with Mary as well as we can Jesus. The only problem with that is it's just not so. You've got to go through Jesus. He is the Mediator, the one Man between people and God is Jesus Christ.

1 John makes it very clear. "He that denies the Son, the same has denied the Father." Ladies and gentlemen, we don't need religious dialogue, we don't need to discuss with all the religions of the world. We don't need to get together and talk about the things we have religiously in common. We need to be twice-born men and women who have had the touch of God upon our souls. We need to tell people of every faith, of every religion, of every creed, of every color who have not known Christ, we need to tell them we have found the answer. His Name is the only Son of God, Jesus Christ.

I remember in Tennessee years ago, there was a young man who wasn't mentally bright and the people there affectionately called him "Dummy." It sounds like disrespect. He could not hear; he could not speak. One summer day they built a brush-arbor meeting and at that first service everybody wondered when "Dummy," the man who couldn't talk and who wasn't mentally bright, would try to make a decision for Christ. He could only make gutteral sounds—unable to speak. On the first invitation, he came down the aisle. Everyone said, "How can he communicate?" Dummy came. There was the Lord's Supper table they had brought out to the brush arbor and there was the large Bible nesting upon that table. When Dummy, who wasn't so dumb after all, came forward he made the only sound he could. He said, "Uhh, uhh." He pointed to the Bible and then to his heart, "Uhh." He pointed to God, "Uhh, uhh, uhh" and they knew he wanted God in his heart.

Dummy got saved. Each night of the revival in that brush arbor Dummy would go back to a man whom everybody knew was lost and would take that man by the shoulder and point to the man's heart and say, "Uhh, uhh, uhh." He wanted God to come into the man's heart and for that man to go down the aisle and accept Christ. Every night of that crusade as the Tennessee people will tell you, Dummy brought somebody to Jesus just by pointing to the man's heart, pointing to the Father in heaven, and pointing the way to the front. Every night, every night.

Later a very affluent man and woman stood to give their testimony in a large Southern Baptist church. Here's the story they told of their getting saved. They said, "Ladies and gentlemen, you won't believe it but about a month ago my wife and I were stopped dead still in a traffic jam. We got out to see what was going on. Cars were lined up this direction and that direction and lined up behind us. We were about seven cars back. My wife and I got out of the car and walked to the intersection to see what we thought must have been a horrible, fatal accident. But we saw something that changed our lives."

They said, and these were their words, "This retarded boy had gone up into the woods and dragged a large timber, a cut pine tree, and dragged it all the way to that intersection. The boy went back into the woods and brought another timber and placed it in that intersection. Dummy had taken two great pine logs, placed them in the intersection in the form of a cross and he would look at everybody getting out of their cars, he would touch their heart and go, 'Uhh, uhh' and then he would point to the cross, 'Uhh, uhh,' and then point to heaven, 'Uhh, uhh.' Ladies and gentlemen, we stood and watched that retarded boy as he would go 'Uhh, uhh,' and then point to that cross, 'Uhh, uhh,' and then point to heaven, 'Uhh, uhh.' We stood and watched that retarded boy as he would go 'Uhh, uhh,' and then point to that cross and go, 'Uhh, uhh' and then he would point to heaven. While we stood there, twenty-one people bowed around those old timbers and gave their hearts to Jesus Christ."

That is the ultimate commitment. May I say finally there is the ultimate success. Jesus said, *My Spirit*. Man is a trichotomy: mind, soul, and body. Jesus said, "I commend my Spirit, I commend my Spirit unto the Father." The ultimate success is one day dying and knowing that we are going to heaven. My friend, Jesus was not headed for the grave, He was headed for heaven. We are not ever going to worry about an airplane, we are just going to have plain air and we are going to rise to meet the Lord. What a glorious day that will be!

I remember reading about the Battle of Waterloo. A man stood on top of a great cathedral in London. He was like a man who stands on a ship, an aircraft carrier, and holds signal flags. This man was wondering if Napoleon could ever be defeated. The whole city of London wanted to know if the Duke of Wellington could do it. And so the man stood on that cathedral and he waved those flags and the people of London came out to get the report of the battle of the Duke of Wellington and Napoleon. When they looked up they could barely see through the fog, but the man, standing on top of that cathedral, was giving the message about the Battle of Waterloo. When the people of England looked, they saw, "Wellington defeated." They could not believe it. All of the hearts of London sank so very low because they saw those two words through the fog: "Wellington defeated."

But I want to tell you something. It wasn't long until that fog abated, it wasn't long until the mists had cleared. The people of London looked again and they saw the entire message which said, "Wellington defeated Napoleon." All of a sudden the entire nation of England rejoiced.

One day when Jesus fought the devil, one day when He climbed Calvary's mountain and shed that blood, there seemed to be one discouraging message to the world, "Christ defeated. Christ defeated. Christ defeated." But I want you to know that when the fog of three days was over, the world learned the truth. The whole message was, "Christ defeated death." Death lost its power. Death lost its sting.

The Bible says that when I stand before God, because of that resurrection power, all nations, tribes, and kindreds will say, "Hallelujah." I went to Kenya, East Africa. They say, "Hallelujah." I could understand it. I've been to Korea and I've heard those people by the thousands say it so I could understand—"Hallelujah." Friend, when we stand before the Lamb of God who takes away the sin of the world, when we stand with Jesus with the nail scars in His hand, in one great chorus of praise, black and white, rich or poor, redeemed by the blood of the Lamb, for eternity our praise will be, "Hallelujah to the King, the Lord God Omnipotent."

9
The Name of Jesus

By Nelson Price

Nelson Lynn Price

Nelson Lynn Price, a native of Osyka, Mississippi, has been pastor of the Roswell Street Baptist Church, Marietta, Georgia, since November 1, 1965. He has served as president of the SBC Pastors' Conference (1987). Formerly he was pastor of Oak Park Baptist Church, New Orleans, Louisiana. His education includes the B.S. degree in horticulture from Southeastern Louisiana University and an M.Div. from New Orleans Baptist Theological Seminary, where he has served many years as a trustee. He has D.D. degrees from Emmanuel School of Theology and Mercer University. His other service to Southern Baptists includes being past president of the Georgia Baptist Convention, a member of the Home Mission Board, SBC, former trustee of Louisiana College, and many other offices. He is the author of eleven books, nine of them Broadman: *How to Find Out Who You Are, I've Got to Play on Their Court, Supreme Happiness, Only the Beginning, The Destruction of Death, Farewell to Fear, Called to Splendor, Shadows We Run From,* and *The Emmanuel Factor; Tenderness and 24 Other Ways to Make a Marriage Work* and *The Occult in Lion Country.* In 1977 he preached the message before President Jimmy Carter's inauguration. His family includes his wife, Trudi, two daughters (now married), Lynn and Sharon, and a grandson.

9
The Name of Jesus

by Nelson Price

Matthew 1:21-23 says Jesus Christ is alive, well, and creatively at work in the lives of His people. I've come to this moment praying that the words of my mouth and the meditations of your hearts will be acceptable in His sight. I thank the Lord for every second to preach about His Name. We are mindful of the value of those seconds and I was particularly made mindful when I heard recently about that reputedly dumb athlete who was failing yet another course. The professor said, "You have one chance to pass it with one last question." It was a question in statistics. The professor made the assignment. "Overnight you have to calculate and come back tomorrow and report. How many seconds are there in a year?" The athlete came in the next day with a big smile saying, "No problem at all. I know the answer to that one." "Great. What is it?" "It was so easy. There are twelve seconds in a year," said the athlete. "Twelve seconds. How did you get that idea?" the professor asked. "Well, it's easy. There is January the second, February the second, March the second."

Well, I'm thankful for every second that is mine to preach

about the Name of Jesus Christ for it is a saving Name. It is a sustaining Name and a sovereign Name. By the instrumentality of the Holy Spirit the Lord breathed through Matthew that Joseph should call Mary's child Jesus for He should save His people from their sin. It's a saving name—the Name of Jesus. John recorded that He was the only begotten of God the Father. That expression "only begotten" translates the Greek word *mono* meaning "one and only," *genes* meaning "the kind." Jesus Christ is the only one of a kind, Son of a God. He is the only God-man, man-God, Jesus Christ being that One. And that's vital.

The issue confronting Christendom today is "What do you believe about this Person and His blessed blood? What do you believe about this Individual and how to relate to Him for there is no mediator between God and persons other than Jesus Christ. On one occasion I was seated in an airplane beside the individual who was at that time the chief labor mediator for President Kennedy. I asked, "What is the characteristic of a mediator?" He said, "A mediator is one who must be equal to both parties." He didn't know I was a minister but he gave the best definition of the mediator Jesus Christ that I have heard for there is no other One who is both equal to God Almighty and to human beings. There is no other Name other than the Name of Jesus whereby ye must be saved. "Call his name Jesus for he shall save his people." It's a selective name. There are those individuals who criticize us for saying, "There is no other name given among men whereby ye must be saved other than the name of Jesus Christ."

But I ask you, is it unfair when a lawyer says to you, "There is only one course of action you can take. There is only one thing you can do that will cause you to win this case. Only one thing that will keep you from being defeated in this lawsuit."?

You wouldn't say of that lawyer, "You are narrow-minded." You would say, "That's great! What is the one thing I can do?" If your doctor said to you, "You have a fatal disease. It is inevitable. It's going to kill you. There is only one thing that can save you." You wouldn't say, "Doctor, you really are narrow-minded." You'd say, "Great, Doc, what is that one thing?" So when the Father says, "There is one way," we should say, "Thank You, Lord, that there is a way."

Is it too narrow to say that water consists of only two molecules of hydrogen and one of oxygen and that it boils only at 112 degrees fahrenheit at sea level? Is it narrow minded to say there are only twelve inches in a foot, only sixteen ounces in a pound, and that A above middle C has 440 vibrations per second, no more and no less? Is that narrow-minded? Nor is it narrow-minded to say there is a Name and the Name is Jesus Christ.

Selectivity, yes. But also the sphere of the saving Name. In the book of 1 Peter, the fifth chapter, the tenth verse, it says that "he has called us to his excellent glory by Christ Jesus." "Called us to his excellent glory." Now that little word *kaleo* which is translated "called" doesn't mean He has called us to heaven, it carries with it the impact of a summons. Thus Peter said, "The Lord God has *summoned* you to heaven." If you know any individual who does not go to heaven, it is because that person turned down the summons of the Lord God Jehovah.

If you've ever received a summons you know what it means. It means to cease and desist in doing whatever you are doing and comply immediately with the requirements of this summons. So God has called us. He's summoned us to heaven. He said, "I want you to get ready and come to be with Me in all eternity." And if any individual does not go to heaven it is be-

cause he or she has first demurred, then delayed, and ulti-
mately denied the summons of the Lord God. That summons
has a scope as broad as the *whosoever* of John 3:16.

I received a letter recently and noticed on the outside a
name that had been very much in the news the days prior to
that—Van Solomon. As I looked at that envelope, I thought
could that possibly be *that* Van Solomon? Opening it, I noticed
that it had been postmarked two days prior to that. It was
written the day before Van Solomon died in the electric chair
here in Georgia. He wrote,

> I want to thank you for telling me on your television program
> yesterday that God loves me and Jesus died for even a person
> like me and that He'd forgive my sin. I've prayed and asked
> Him to cleanse me and to save my soul, and I just want some-
> body to know. I'm ready to meet Him.

In the Name of Jesus that redemption occurred. Since that
time I have received correspondence from others there on
death row. One recently said, "I'd like for you to know that
nineteen of the twenty-six of us here on death row now have
gotten the message you've been preaching to us and because of
the Name of Jesus we are ready to go meet the Father." The
Name of Jesus is a redemptive Name. For every prisoner in our
jails today it costs our government seventeen-thousand dollars
a year. It costs only fifteen-thousand dollars to send a student
to Harvard. If you add up all the dollars that all the Baptist
churches in America received in a recent year and you divide
those dollars by the number of converts all our churches reported in that same year, you'd find that it cost eleven-
thousand dollars per soul saved through our Baptist churches.

Do you get the picture? It's cheaper to save them than it is to
incarcerate them. It is cheaper to save them than it is to exe-

cute them. It is cheaper to get an individual into heaven for all of eternity than it is to get a child through Harvard for one single year. Thank God for the saving Name of Jesus Christ.

Likewise as you move further into the Bible to the book of Hebrews, the second chapter, in that fifteenth verse you find this great truth that the Lord God hath delivered them who through fear all of their lives were subject to bondage. *Subject to bondage* translates an expression that describes an animal caught in a snare and unable to free itself. It is like the insect caught in the spider's web. The moment that insect hits that web, it is affixed and attached. The more it struggles to save itself the more entwined and the more captive it becomes. Self efforts of salvation are insufficient. The spider can tarry and toy with the insect until finally at last that paralyzing poison is injected into the body of the insect. The spider delays as long as desired before devouring it.

Any individual you know without the Lord Jesus Christ as personal Savior is caught in the death web. Only Jesus Christ can save and deliver individuals from that death web. The name Jesus Christ is a saving Name. Further in the book of Matthew, the first chapter, the twenty-third verse, therein it is said, ". . . you shall call His name Emmanuel," which means "God with us." Emmanuel. I thank God that He is with us—His presence.

I have a friend who is a businessman here in Atlanta with offices in 150 American cities. As a part of the employment process they give a polygraph test to all would-be employees. The businessman told me that the person who gives this polygraph test recently gave him a signed affidavit in which he said, "I always ask potential employees, 'Do you believe there is a God?'" And he said every avowed atheist who answered "No, I don't believe there is a God" has been shown on that polygraph to be lying. Even the disavowing are not disbelieving. We who profess to believe should be professing because of His presence and His power with us.

He has the power to meet the needs in your life. He has the power to meet you right where you are and to give you the strength that you need. Jesus Christ said to Simon Peter in the garden when Simon drew the sword and wanted to defend Him, He said, "Peter, don't you know that I could have prayed to My Father and He would have sent more than seventy-two thousand angels." I know the song says ten-thousand angels but the Book says more than seventy-two thousand angels. As you read in your Old Testament you will find there was one angel that on one occasion killed more than 185,000 people. That meant that at the moment Jesus Christ faced Calvary for your sin and my sin, He had at His immediate disposal the kill power of 13,750,000,000 but He restrained the power in order that he might manifest a greater power and that is the power that saves your soul and my soul by His shed blood.

I thank God that He's got the power to meet our needs. His is a sustaining Name, the Name Jesus Christ. You may be an individual in the hour of present extremity. You may be in a congregation where members have promised you over and over again that they will support you, they will work with you and time and again you've found yourself boxed in or boxed out. You find yourself in an impossible position. You find yourself on occasion in honesty on your knees praying to the Lord God and saying, "Oh, dear Heavenly Father, I feel like You are not here with me now"—because you really don't.

But the reason you may feel that way is because you may have been in some long committee meeting the night before. It was a long, hot, dry ride through ulcer gulch and you don't feel like God is with you. But then you can come back to His

Word in which He said, "I will never leave you. I will never forsake you. I will be with you always even to the end of the world" (author's paraphrase). Then you can say, "Lord, I don't feel like You are here with me but I thank You that in Your Book You said You would always be with me in spite of the feelings. I thank You for the fact You are here, Lord. You are here and because You are, let's You and I go get 'em today." He's got the power to meet your need and He will do it if you will allow Him to.

In your life, in my life, in all our lives we have crises and He is present with us. He is Emmanuel. You can find Him there in the hour of need. You have physical extremities, therefore I have no timidity about sharing one of my own with you. It was the Christmas season. We had had a party at our home that evening and the guests had all left. It was now 2:30 AM and I heard a sound in our lower part of the house. Thinking some of the guests must still be there, I went downstairs to find that lower floor of our house a blazing inferno. I tried as best I could for a few minutes to put it out before it consumed the house and perhaps us with it. Without success I retreated through the house calling out to my family, telling them the house was on fire. I ran outside, broke out windows, and started trying to put water on the fire with a hose.

As the fire department arrived I started to walk away and when I did I realized for the first time that when I had been in that room the carpet had blazed up and was nothing but molten carpet. I had been standing in molten carpet and now, as I turned to walk away, I was literally pulling the soles of my feet. They scooped me up, put my feet in the saline solution, took me to the emergency room. The doctor said, "We've got to strip the flesh off your feet. We can't give you an anesthetic. It may put you in shock. We've got to do it without an anesthetic." In the moments that followed I had two options—scream and cry, or laugh and praise God. I never did like to cry so I grabbed the rails of the bed, twisted and bent them, and laughed and praised God for His presence even in moment of physical agony.

I've been in the fire. You've been in the fire. I've been in the fire and the Fourth Man was there. I've been in the wilderness and there is a Way out of there. I've had my back against the wall and there is a Door there. I've been to the well and there is Water there. I've been in the darkness and there is a Light there. His Name is Jesus.

It's a Saving Name. It's a Sustaining Name. It's a Sovereign Name. Philippians 2:9-11 says,

> God also hath . . . given Him a name which is above very name, that at the name of Jesus every knee should bow, of things in heaven, and things in earth, and things under the earth; and that every tongue should confess that Jesus Christ is Lord, to the glory of God the Father.

At His advent, the Father said, "His Name is Jesus." At His ascension and accession to the throne the Father said, "His Name is Lord." Lord. . . *Kurios* in the Greek. The word was used in a variety of ways. I shall give you three ways in which *Kurios*—Lord—was used. It was used as a title of respect very much like we use the word "sir" or "ma'am" in the South. It was used as a title of authority, such as a lord over a vineyard. It was also used as a title for deity. The Romans referred to Caesar as *Kurios*, believing him to be God. So when you say *Lord* you are really saying, "O dear God, the One whose authority in my life I respect." "Lord," the One I'm sold out to, the One I call Savior, the One I submit to as Sovereign. It is a

Saving Name. It's a Sustaining Name. And it is a Sovereign Name—the Name Jesus.

What are you going to do with it? Preach it. Preach it with gratitude for the joy of preaching it. Preach the Name Jesus. It is a wonderful Name. Preach it—

> Preach by your lives, and preach from the Word:
> Preach by your singing, that souls may be stirred.
>
> Preach on a trolley or preach on a bus;
> Preach without fanfare and preach without fuss:
>
> Preach in a hall or preach in a shack;
> Preach the Word and never turn back.
>
> Preach on the sidewalk, preach the "Good News";
> Preach the Gospel and not men's views.
>
> Preach with the unction the Holy Spirit imparts;
> Preach to touch lives and melt cold hearts.
>
> Preach only Christ, the Savior of men;
> Tell how He died, and liveth again.
>
> Preach the pure Gospel, so true and so tried;
> Preach casting all doubts and false doctrine aside.
>
> Preach every moment till life's race is run;
> Preach till in Heaven you hear His "well done."
> —Jennie E. Hussey

Preach the Name Jesus.

10
Is There Any Hope?

By James Reimer

James Reimer

James Reimer, native of Indianapolis, has been pastor of Second Baptist Church, Springfield, Missouri, since 1982. He was formerly pastor of the Baptist Tabernacle, Atlanta, Georgia, Emmanuel Baptist Church, Enid, Oklahoma, First Baptist Church, Jackson Lake, Texas, and Foxworthy Baptist Church, San Jose, California. He was educated at California Baptist College in Riverside (B.A.) and Southwestern Baptist Theological Seminary, Fort Worth, Texas. His family includes his wife, Kathleen, and three children, Mark, Lisa, and Jennifer.

10
Is There Any Hope?

by James Reimer

Would you take out your hymn book and turn to 1 Peter. That's what it is, you know. It's a book about *Him*. A *Him* Book. It's a book about the Lord Jesus Christ. I've found Him on every page of the Word of God. So open your Him Book to 1 Peter, chapter 1, verse 3.

> Blessed be the God and Father of our Lord Jesus Christ, which according to his abundant mercy hath begotten us again into a lively hope by the resurrection of Jesus Christ from the dead.

During World War II, an American submarine was torpedoed by a Nazi U-boat off the coast of England. A distress signal was sent out from that sinking submarine. The Allied forces picked it up, and immediately a rescue ship was dispatched. When the rescue ship arrived at the scene, they found only an oil slick and some floating debris to mark the place where the submarine had been attacked. Immediately the ship sent divers down to the sunken submarine to see if they could find any sign of life. When the divers got down to the submarine, they began to swim around it. They took out their knives and with the hands of the knives they began to tap on the steel wall, thinking that perhaps they would get a response from someone who might still be alive. As one of the divers was tapping on the side of that submarine, he heard a responding tapping from inside. He grew excited and he began to tap again. Again he received a tap from inside.

Then the diver noticed that there seemed to be a pattern to the tapping. He recognized it. It was Morse Code. Someone inside the submarine was tapping out a message in Morse Code. The diver listened as the message was tapped out. These are the words that the person in the submarine tapped out: "Is there any hope?" Is there any hope?"

It seems to me that that is the desperate question of our sunken society. Our society has been torpedoed by the enemy Satan and has sunk to the bottom of a sea of sensuality, a sea of sin, a sea of secularism. Our society has sunk to the bottom of the ocean of immorality, an ocean of humanism, an ocean of materialism. I believe that from the depths our world is crying out to us, "Is there any hope?"

Perhaps many of you have come to Atlanta with this very same question. Deep down your heart cries out, "Is there any hope? Is there any hope for our Convention? Is there any hope for my church? Is there any hope for my ministry? Is there any hope for my marriage? Is there any hope for me?"

The apostle Peter wrote in the words of our text that because of the resurrection of Jesus Christ, there *is* hope. I believe that today. I believe that no matter how desperate the situation, I believe that no matter how difficult the circumstances, I believe that no matter how dark the condition, there is hope. There is hope because Jesus is a risen, reigning Lord and I want us to see that hope. I want us to see that lively hope our resurrected Lord brings to us. I want us to leave this conference with this lively hope burning fresh and new in our hearts.

I want you to notice the four desperate situations to which the resurrected Christ gives hope. First of all, the resurrected Christ gives hope to those who weep in death. John told us in his gospel that Mary Magdalene came early in the morning to the tomb of Jesus and that she stood outside the sepulcher weeping. Mary was the last one at the cross and the first one at the tomb. Mary desperately loved Jesus. Mark tells us why—it was out of Mary Magdalene the Lord Jesus had cast seven demons. So she loved Him deeply and she came to that tomb early in the morning. I believe she came to be near Him somehow. I believe that for some reason she could not bear to let Him go. She could not bear to give Him up, like all of us who have had loved ones pass away.

I heard a story about a woman who was dying of a terminal illness. The doctor came to visit her and to examine her and when he finished the examination he said, "I must tell you truthfully that you have only a few months to live. I would suggest that you prepare yourself and your son, Tommy, for your sure demise." The woman said, "But doctor, I just don't know what to say to my son. I just don't know how to tell him. Doctor, would you help me?" The doctor answered, "Yes, I'll do that. Where is he?" She replied, "He's out in the backyard playing."

So the doctor folded up his black bag and went out into the backyard and he said, "Tommy, come here, Son." Little Tommy came over and the doctor put his arm around him and they sat down. The doctor said, "Son, I've got something to tell you. Your mother will soon be going away. And when she goes away, Tommy, she's not ever going to come back." The little boy looked at the doctor and asked, "What do you mean, Doctor?" The doctor said, "Well, it's like this. Your mother is going to go on a long trip and it is such a far trip that when she goes she is not ever going to come back." The little boy said, "Well, Doctor, when does she have to go away?"

The doctor was trying to give him some idea of when it was going to be and so he looked up at the tree and said, "Tommy, do you see the leaves on this tree?" Tommy said, "Yes sir." The doctor said, "Tommy, when all the leaves are gone from that tree, your mama is going to go away and she is not ever going to come back home."

So the doctor left. A couple of months later he came back by the home to once again examine the woman who was failing and was almost at the point of death. The doctor said to her, "How is Tommy doing?" She said, "I don't know. I don't see him very much. He spends most of his time out back playing. Doctor, before you leave would you talk to him again?" He said, "Yes, I'll do that."

The doctor went back out into the backyard and he looked for Tommy but he couldn't find him. He said, "Tommy, Tommy, where are you?" He heard the voice of little Tommy coming from a tree up above him. He looked up and there was Tommy in the tree. He said, "Tommy, Son, what are you doing up in the tree?" Little Tommy said, "I'm tying these leaves to these branches."

You see, we don't want to let them go. We do everything we can to cling to them but there comes a time when we've got to let them go. There comes a time in our lives when we've got to turn them loose. There comes a time when that dear old daddy has to slip out into eternity to meet God. There comes a time when that sweet, precious mother whom we've loved all these years will die. We've got to turn loose and let them go into eternity to meet our Lord. It is so much easier to let them go and turn them loose when we know Jesus who is the Resurrection and the Life because Jesus gives us hope for those who weep in death.

Dr. George W. Truett told a story about a funeral he once conducted for a beautiful little six-year-old girl who had tragically died. Her mother was a wonderful Christian and a member of his church but her father was not a Christian. Dr. Truett talked about how sad that funeral was. When he finished the funeral message he walked down and stood beside the casket. The casket was open and the people came by and looked at the beautiful little girl lying there in that silk-lined casket. Finally the daddy came. That great big, hulking he-man. He came to the casket, held onto the edge of it as his hands trembled, tears streaming down his cheeks as he looked at the cold, lifeless form of his precious little baby girl. He looked at her and he said, "Oh, my baby, you are gone. You are gone. Gone. Goodby forever." Then he turned and walked away.

Then Dr. Truett said that sweet little mother came to the casket. She stood there and reached over and with her finger she twirled one of those little blonde curls. She reached and straightened the ruffle on the little girl's dress and then reached over and kissed her cold cheek. The mother said, "My darling, you've only been with us for six years but these have been six wonderful, joyous years and now my precious little one, I say to you, 'Goodnight' because Mama will see you and our Lord in the morning." One came to the casket and said "Goodby." The other came to the casket and said "Goodnight." You see, that's the difference Jesus makes. He is the Resurrection and the Life and there is hope for those who weep in death.

Second, there is hope for those who worry in dismay. John

told us in his Gospel that after Jesus' death His disciples were hiding behind closed doors for fear of the Jews. They had sequestered and secluded themselves. The doors were bolted and the windows locked. They were talking to each other in hushed tones because they were afraid. They were fearful. They were anxious. I wonder, how many of us are just like that? How many pastors are worried? How many anxious? Fearful? Afraid? I wonder, truthfully, how many men are afraid perhaps of some person who is very powerful in their church. They are afraid perhaps of their deacons. They are afraid perhaps of their finance committee, the personnel committee, or the church treasurer. Just like the disciples, perhaps you are fearful. I believe we fear because like the disciples we only realize the death of Jesus and we have not fully realized the power of His resurrected presence.

I want you to know that no matter how tough it is, no matter how rough it is, no matter how dark it is, the Lord Jesus walks with you. Alexander Maclaren, that great Scottish preacher, once told a story about himself. He said when he was sixteen years old he got his first job in the city of Glasgow. He lived with his family out on a farm about six or eight miles from the city. He would go to work in the city all week long, stay there, and then walk home on the weekends to be with his family. Now between the farmhouse where his family lived and the city of Glasgow was a very deep, dark, and forbidding ravine. In that ravine many people had been attacked, mugged, robbed, and some had even been killed. He was deathly afraid of that dark ravine and so Monday morning when his daddy walked him into the city, he said to him as he walked away, "Alex, Son, when you get off work on Friday afternoon, I want you to come home immediately because this is going to be a long week for me and your mother. We're not used to being apart from you so come on home Friday."

Alexander Maclaren thought about that deep, dark valley and how he must walk through it on Friday night. He said, "Well, Dad, I'm going to be really tired from working all week long. What I'd like to do is just stay in the city Friday night and just walk on home on Saturday morning." His dad said, "No, Son, no we're going to miss you too much. I want you to come home Friday night." He said, "Alright, Dad." Alexander Maclaren said he worked all week long in fear and dread of walking throughout that dark valley on Friday night. He was so fearful, so anxious, and afraid.

Finally Friday came and he packed his belongings, got out on the road, and began to walk down the dark road. As he walked, he whistled to keep up his courage. He talked out loud to an imaginary companion on the way. Finally he came to the edge of that dark ravine. Tears welled up in his eyes. He just couldn't bring himself to walk down into that dark, dark valley alone. As he stood there he heard something . . . something was stirring down in that ravine. He was paralyzed with fear. He couldn't run, he couldn't do anything.

He looked and up out of that ravine came the face and figure of the man whom he loved most on earth. It was his daddy. His father said, "Alex, I missed you so much and I came out here to meet you to walk home with you." Alexander Maclaren said that that night, shoulder to shoulder and side by side, he and his father walked down into that dark, dark valley and out the other side and he was not afraid because his father was with him.

I don't know what dark ravine you might be walking through but I know Jesus said, "I'll never leave you nor forsake you. I won't leave you comfortless. I will come to you and I will walk with you through those dark valleys. I will take those dark valleys away and I will remove those difficult situations. I'll be your Companion and I'll be your Comforter along the way. Through it all My grace will be sufficient." There is hope for those who weep in death. There is hope for those who worry in dismay.

Third, there is hope for those who wonder in doubt. When the risen Lord Jesus first appeared to His disciples, one of His disciples was absent. It was Thomas. You see, Thomas wasn't there because Thomas had become disillusioned. Thomas had become disturbed. Thomas had started to doubt because his world had fallen apart. The bottom had dropped out and Thomas had come to a time in his life when he didn't know what he believed anymore. He had come to a time when he doubted his calling. He doubted his commitment. He doubted Christ . . . he doubted everything.

Perhaps some of you who are here today are like that, you have come to that place in your life. Maybe you've come to a time when you really don't know what to believe anymore. You've come to a time when you are wandering aimlessly in doubt and confusion. Maybe you've come to doubt your commitment, maybe you've come to doubt your calling. Maybe you've come to doubt Christ.

I want you to know that there is hope because the second time Jesus appeared to His disciples Thomas was there with all of his skepticism, cynicism, doubts, and questions. Thomas was there. Suddenly Jesus appeared in their midst. Did you ever notice how Jesus dealt with Thomas, the doubter? Did you ever notice what He said? He dealt with him so differently than we would do. When Jesus saw Thomas, He didn't say, "Well, there you are, Doubter." He didn't say, "I told you I was going to rise from the grave and you didn't believe Me. You doubted, so get out of My sight."

No, the resurrected Lord Jesus in His tenderness, love, and compassion came to Thomas. He said, "Thomas, here, reach out your finger and touch. See where the marks are. See where they drove the nails. Here, Thomas, come over here and put your hand in My side and see where the spear was." And when the Lord Jesus did that, Thomas fell on his knees and said, "My Lord and my God." From that moment he experienced the resurrected Christ. He never doubted again. It will cure your doubts every time.

Do you know what people need who wander in doctrinal doubt? What they need is an encounter with the resurrected Lord because He will cure your doubts. Do you have doubts today? Take them to Jesus.

One day Robert Ingersoll, the noted infidel, was riding on a train with General Lew Wallace, who was an author. Ingersoll challenged Wallace to write a book that would once and for all show the claims of the Gospel to be ludicrous, to be mythical. Lew Wallace accepted the challenge, but to write the book he had to first research the Bible. So he began to read very carefully the Gospel narratives. He began to study about the life, death, and resurrection of Jesus. While he was researching the gospel, Wallace became overwhelmingly convinced that Jesus Christ did in fact rise from the grave. He subsequently wrote the novel *Ben-Hur*.

There *is* hope! There is hope for those who weep in death, for those who worry in dismay, for those who wonder in doubt and, finally, there is hope for those who walk in denial.

Simon Peter said that he would never deny Jesus and yet he did it three times. Three times he cursed, three times he swore. Did you ever notice that Simon Peter, who denied the Lord

Jesus that day, later on was greatly used of the Lord Jesus? Did you ever notice that at the tomb the angel told Mary this: he said, "Go and tell the disciples and Peter to meet Him in Galilee." Notice he said, "And Peter." Why was Peter singled out? Why was Peter especially named?

I'll tell you. Simon Peter didn't think he was a disciple anymore. Simon Peter felt he had so sinned, that he had so failed the Lord that he had forfeited his discipleship, that he had forfeited his ministry. He felt he would never ever be qualified to serve Jesus again.

But John ended that last wonderful chapter of his Gospel, chapter 21 where Jesus encountered Peter on the banks there of that lake. Jesus said to Peter, "Peter, do you love Me? Do you really love Me?" And Peter said, "Yes, Lord. You know all things. You know I love You." Jesus said, "Peter even though you denied Me, even though you sinned, I want you to serve Me and feed My sheep." You see, Jesus forgave him and reinstated him. Jesus used him again as the mighty, powerful preacher of Pentecost.

Maybe today you are here and you feel like Simon Peter. Maybe you feel that for some reason or other you have failed your Lord. Maybe some sin has suddenly crept into your life and you've committed some sin that perhaps you thought you would never commit and maybe you feel unworthy to serve Him and you feel like you have forfeited your ministry. Listen, I want you to know that there is hope for those who walk in denial. For John told us in 1 John 1:9, "If we confess our sins, he is faithful and just to forgive our sins, and to cleanse us from all unrighteousness."

There is hope today for broken promises. There is hope today for broken preachers because God forgives us, cleanses us, reinstates us, and uses us again. The Ark of the Covenant was the most holy and sacred piece of furniture in the temple. It was a golden chest that resided in the Holy of Holies behind a curtain. On top of the Ark of the Covenant was a golden slab called the Mercy Seat. On the Mercy Seat was poised an angel, one on each end. Once a year the High Priest on Yom Kippur would come with the bowl of blood. He would go beyond the veil and there on the Mercy Seat he would take the bowl of blood drawn from the spotless lamb and pour it out onto the Mercy Seat so that God in His Shekinah Presence could no longer see the broken laws in the chest. They were covered and thus an atonement was made and sins were forgiven.

Do you know what John told us in his Gospel? When Mary came to the sepulcher and looked in, do you know what John said she saw? Not only did she see the stone slab bloody from where the Lord Jesus had lain. But John wrote that there was an angel at the head and one at the feet of the place where the body of Jesus had lain. I believe that somehow God had moved the Mercy Seat from the temple to the tomb. He moved it from the Holy of Holies to the hole in the rock because that is where our sins are forgiven, because Jesus died on the cross and rose victorious from the tomb. Our sins past, present, and future are all forgiven. There *is* hope.

In 1488 the Cape of South Africa was discovered by Bartholemew Diaz. It was a very dangerous place. It was very treacherous because of the different turbulent ocean currents. When he sailed around the Cape of South Africa, he named it the Cape of Storms. But just a few years later in 1497, Vasco de Gama sailed around that cape and he discovered a new trade route from Europe to India. When he came back to Portugal, he reported to the King: "No longer will that cape be called the Cape of Storms. Now it will be called the Cape of Good Hope."

You see, the cross and death of Jesus looked like the Cape of Storms. It looked like the place of death. It looked like the place of destruction. But on the third day Jesus rose from that tomb and now it is no longer the Cape of Storms, it is now the Cape of Good Hope. God has begotten us unto a lively hope by the resurrection of Jesus.

There is hope for those who weep in death, there is hope for those who worry in dismay, there is hope for those who wonder in doubt, there is hope for those who walk in denial.

Michaelangelo, the great Renaissance artist, once chided his contemporary artists. He said to them one day, "Why do you always paint Jesus on the cross? Why do you not rather paint Him standing at the open tomb? Why do you always paint Him as the victim? Why do you not rather paint Him as the Victor?"

There is hope because Jesus is alive and risen forevermore.

11
Anointed to Preach Jesus

By Dwight "Ike" Reighard

Dwight "Ike" Reighard

Dwight "Ike" Reighard serves as pastor of the New Hope Baptist Church, Fayetteville, Georgia. He is a graduate of Mercer University and holds the D.D. degree from Luther Rice Seminary. He and his wife, Robin, have one daughter, Abigail. He served as secretary-treasurer of the 1986 Pastors' Conference (SBC).

11
Anointed to Preach Jesus

by Dwight "Ike" Reighard

This is a marvelous opportunity for me because right out in front of the World Congress Center there is a street called Marietta Street. That's the street where I grew up. I did not have the opportunity of growing up in a Christian family. I did not grow up in a Christian environment but I was saved when I was nearly twenty-one years old. A youth minister in a church nearby led me to a saving knowledge of the Lord Jesus Christ. He told me that the Bible is God's inerrant, infallible Word. I believed it then and I believe it now. If I'm going to preach Jesus, if I'm going to be anointed, then I've got to believe the Book.

I heard a story one time about a lady who was reading her Bible while riding on a train. A gentleman looked over at her and asked, "Do you believe all the things that are in that book?" She said, "I certainly do." He said, "You mean you believe all the stories that are located in the Bible?" She said, "Why certainly." He said, "Well, what about when Jonah was swallowed by the great big fish. Do you mean to tell me you believe that?" She said, "Yes, certainly." He said, "But you look so educated. How could you believe a fable like that . . . that Jonah could live in the belly of that fish for three days?" She said, "Mister, if God's Word says it, I believe it." He persisted and said, "Tell me, why do you believe it?" She said, "I don't know exactly how Jonah lived in that fish for three days, but when I get to heaven I'll ask Jonah." He said, "But lady, what if Jonah's not in heaven?" She said, "Then you ask him." I believe the Bible is God's inerrant, infallible Word.

In 1 Samuel, chapter 16, the Bible tells us about my favorite character in the Scripture. I think every preacher really feels a kinship with King David. There was something about David that just makes us love him so much. He's that little shepherd boy who goes from living out in the fields to living in palaces. He's the young man who goes from living with the sheep to becoming king over all of Israel. He's the young man who goes from rags to riches. He is what we would call today the American dream.

In 1 Samuel, chapter 16, there is recorded the reason for David's immense success. It is found in verse 12 of 1 Samuel, chapter 16. The prophet Samuel had gone to the house of Jesse and he asked Jesse, "Jesse, God told me to come here and to anoint the next king over all of Israel. He's going to be one of your sons." I imagine Jesse was amazed by that because he was just an ordinary man with an ordinary family but God was going to do something extraordinary with this man's life and in his family.

So he paraded all of his sons before Samuel, the prophet, and Samuel looked at them as they marched past. There was one young man whom he really thought would be the next king. He seemed to stand head and shoulders above all the rest and his name was Eliab. Samuel immediately said in his own heart, "This is the man." But then God spoke to him and the

Lord said to Samuel, "Do not look at his appearance or his height because I've rejected him." God sees not as man sees for man looks at the outward appearance but the Lord looks at the heart.

And Samuel said, "Jesse, do you have any other sons?" Jesse said, "Well, I've got one last son. He's the runt of the litter. He's out there in the fields." Samuel said, "Well, we'll not eat, we'll not sacrifice until I see this young man." And these are the verses that are recorded when David walked into the presence of this mighty prophet of God.

> And he sent, and brought him in. Now he was ruddy, with beautiful eyes and a handsome appearance. And the Lord said to the heart of Samuel, Arise, anoint him: for this is he. Then Samuel took the horn of oil, and anointed him in the midst of his brothers: and the Spirit of the Lord came mightily upon David from that day forward (author's paraphrase).

In our generation we need anointed preaching. Where there is anointed preaching, there is going to be soul-winning. They go together. I've never seen a church get into a fight if that church was a soul-winning church. She's too busy majoring on the main business to get sidetracked onto something else. We have the opportunity to say, "Lord, I want to be a Spirit-anointed preacher so that when I stand in the pulpit people will hear more than just an echo. They will hear the voice of God. I honestly believe we could change America if people hear a word from God when we preach.

Dr. Vance Havner, in his book *Hearts Afire*, told of being in a Los Angeles hotel. He said when he woke up that morning he looked out and smog covered the city, He said he turned on the weather forecast and the weatherman said, "There is a weather alert out today because the smog is so thick. It's going to remain over the city for the next few days unless a wind from elsewhere blows away the smog." A wind from elsewhere.

Dr. Havner went on to say that if revival ever comes to the Southern Baptist Convention, if revival ever sweeps across the thirty-six thousand churches of our convention, it will happen when the wind from elsewhere blows across our churches. Until then we are going to be powerless. Until then we may see some pockets of revival, but what we need in this world is a Holy Ghost revival. Four billion people in the world are counting on us. Southern Baptists, the largest Protestant denomination in the world with over fourteen million people, must get back to the main business of winning people to Jesus.

As pastors we need to understand today that the wind from elsewhere is the breath of the Almighty God that sweeps across our congregations. You see, without God-breathed wind, our preaching is just going to be the words of mankind rather than the work of the Master.

Pastors, what do you face every Sunday morning when you stand in your pulpit to preach to your people? Sometimes pastors get frustrated but we need to understand what we are facing when we stand to preach.

For instance, in a typical congregation there may be a woman sitting over on the righthand side close to the front down near the altar who just lost her husband of fifty years. He's gone to be with the Lord.

Near the back perhaps there is a couple who is facing an impending divorce. Both husband and wife are looking and praying for some last hope that may save their marriage.

Over in the middle maybe there is a woman who desperately desires God's direction. She wants to know what God desires her to do and she is there to get an answer.

On the right at the end of the pew is possibly a young man

who's been called to preach but at the moment he is going through a crisis in his faith as he tries to obtain a higher education. Many of the things he has come to believe have put him in a crisis of his faith and he wants to know how his faith can be solidified once again.

On the left possibly is a senior adult who just got the news yesterday that the biopsy which came back from the hospital is malignant.

There is another young couple who is there and this young man and woman are going to be married soon. They want to know how to make their marriage one which will be built upon the Rock.

And then down at the front, a nine-year-old boy is sitting, drawing on a piece of paper, and getting ready to hear the preacher. When it comes time to preach we stand in the pulpit and open up the Word of God for all of these different people in an effort to meet their unique and varying needs.

If the only wind that blows across that congregation is the breath of the preacher, or a burst of air from an air-conditioner, then those people are going to go away with their needs unmet and their lives unchanged. But, if the wind from elsewhere blows across your congregation, what miracles will take place!

For instance, those who are lonely will feel like they are loved. Those who have questions will get the answers and we just marvel that one sermon will meet one need in one person's life and a totally opposite need in another life. The fearful will get their faith. The beauty of it all is that the lost will get saved.

You see, when the breath of God, the wind from elsewhere, blows across that congregation, there is a vitality and there is life that no one can ever manufacture. The question I want to ask every pastor is why do we settle for the counterfeit when we can have the real thing? Why do we settle for the counterfeit? Why do we go up there to win them with the funny jokes and the cute stories to entice the people to love us? Why don't we get so saturated with the Word of God that when we stand to preach, the people know they have a Word from God. That's what we need across our Southern Baptist Convention.

Here are three ways I believe that can happen. Three questions for us to ask ourselves. Number one, why should my preaching be anointed? In Isaiah, chapter 61, verses 1-2, I believe God gives us the answer. He says that our preaching should be anointed because the

> Spirit of the Lord God is upon me; because the Lord hath anointed me to preach good tidings unto the meek: he hath sent me to bind up the broken-hearted, to proclaim liberty to the captives, and the opening of the prison to them that are bound; To proclaim the acceptable year of the Lord, and the day of vengeance of our God; to comfort all that mourn.

You see, God commands us to be anointed of Him so that we will have power when we stand in the pulpit. That is God's anointing; that we will have pathos when we stand in the pulpit; that we will see the broken-hearted healed. But we'll also have precision in our preaching because we'll be able to proclaim the favorable year of our Lord.

The reason why our preaching should be anointed is because God commands it in His Word. If we are going to follow after the example of our Lord Jesus Christ, then our preaching must be anointed. But our preaching also ought to be anointed because the human condition requires it. You see, "all we like sheep have gone astray." The Bible says there is not one that has not sinned and come short of the glory of God. If we do not proclaim the gospel to all people, then they are going to be lost and they are going to be separated from God. They are going to go to an eternity in hell and I believe in a literal hell as I believe in a literal heaven. That's why I preach. That's why I try to win people because I believe what God's Word says about it. The human condition requires it.

But you know, it's remarkable in our day and age how many people really question that. I just did a talk show in Atlanta on Friday and the host of that show said, "You know, I've got one problem with all you preachers." I said, "What's that?" He said, "The fact that you are always calling us sinners. Why do you always call us sinners?" I said, "Well, because that is what the Bible teaches; that without Christ we are dead in our trespasses and in our sin. I say that because of what God's Word says."

Then he gave me a perfect lead-in. He said, "Preacher, do you mean to tell me that when you go out to a hospital and you look at all those tiny infants there that you believe they have sin in their lives?" I said, "I certainly do because I believe in a literal Adam and Eve and I believe that by one man's sin, sin came into the world and yes, I do believe we are born in iniquity, we are born in sin." He said, "Well, that seems so barbaric."

I said, "Can I ask you a question?" He said, "Certainly." I said, "Well, tell me. You have children. Let me ask you this question. When was the last time you had to teach your child how to be bad?" You say, "You don't have to teach them how to be bad." Why not? Because it just comes naturally. You see, our condition requires it.

We have people in our airport who are sharing a false gospel. They are trying to share something that's not even true and yet we say we believe Christ when He says He is the Way, the Truth and the Life. Those people are often working harder than any of us dare to work. We must have our preaching anointed because Christ commands it and because our condition requires it.

But how can my preaching be anointed? I mean, all of us would love to be able to stand and preach and to have the anointing like Billy Graham. What makes the difference when God blesses one man so much and one church is growing in such a great way and yet right down the street it seems as if everything is going downhill? Well, I believe from the life of David we discover a few things that will show us how our preaching can be anointed.

Number one, you've got to have preparation. You see, David was faithful in the things unseen and he was rewarded in the open. Little became much because David was willing to be out there with the sheep and to do the task that his father gave to him. Are we willing to prepare our sermons the way we should or does sermon preparation just become something tacked onto the end of a very busy week? You see, laziness is a contradiction to the call to preach and laziness is not a product of your hormones. It is something you have chosen to do. One of the problems we have is that we become lazy in preparation and we plan on somebody else doing our sermons for us. If we do that then all we do when we stand to preach is just become an echo of what some other man teaches or what some other man preaches. We need to prepare.

Not only must we have preparation that will make our preaching anointed, but also we must have purity in our lives. You see, the Bible says that David was a man after God's own heart "who will do all my will." That's the way Paul described him in the book of Acts. That means that God has a heart, that we have a heart, and the secret to anointed preaching is to make God's heart our heart. It's amazing when we can make God's heart our heart. The cleaner you become in your personal life, the clearer your sermons are going to be if you seek to be that pure man of God.

There is nothing in the world that I think would be more embarrassing or disheartening than to stand before God someday and for God to look at us and say, "Here's what I wanted to do with your life but here's the cheap substitute which you chose." You see, Saul was the man who had been anointed to be king over all of Israel but Samuel went to him one day and said, "Saul, God has taken the kingdom away from you. God has taken it away from you because you would not seek after Him. He's taken it from you and He's given it to a man who is after His own heart."

In every era, in every period of time, God searches for the man who really wants His heart. So you see, how can my preaching be anointed? Well, I'm going to have to have the preparation. I'm going to have to take the time. I'm going to have to have purity in my life. If I want power in my works, then I must be pure before God. But also, the purpose in your life is important. You see, David did not seek to be the leader. David sought after God's own heart and God did all the rest. If we'll learn to put God first in our lives, He'll do the rest, and we should not seek God to accomplish our end.

So not only do we have a purpose that will help us be Spirit-filled preachers, but also we must have a prayer in our lives because prayer is what strikes the winning blow. Pastor, how much time do you spend praying each day? Christian layperson, how much time do you spend praying? We want God to shake our buildings and the power of heaven to fall, and we give Him two minutes of prayer half-heartedly. There's no way God can bless that kind of praying. You see, true preaching is what Jesus and I talk about all week long as we pray together. That's what true preaching is all about.

So David went out and he had the power of God on his life. That's how we can be anointed by God. But here's another question. When will your preaching be anointed? When will it really be anointed? Number one, it will be anointed when you have a true allegiance to the One in authority. If you have a true allegiance *to* the One in authority, then you are going to have a true allegiance *from* the One in authority. Do you think for a moment that God wants your pulpit to be a powerless place? Do you think for one moment that God wants your pulpit to be void of people coming to know Jesus Christ as their personal Lord and Savior? Surely not. He gave His Son to give you that kind of power and He resurrected Him from the grave to give you the impetus, to give you that power of the Holy Spirit in your life to be able to stand and to preach that Word of God. Do you have a true allegiance *to* the One in authority? If you do, you'll have a true allegiance *from* the One in authority.

But what kind of allegiance are we talking about? What does our allegiance consist of? I think it's two things. Number one, there's no way you can be a Spirit-anointed preacher unless you believe the Word of God. I don't think there is any way you can do it. I don't think you can fabricate it.

David Hulme was a British philosopher. He rejected historic Christianity. One day he was hurrying down a London street. A friend asked him where he was going. He said, "I'm going to hear the preacher, George Whitfield." The friend looked at him astonished and said, "But surely you don't believe what Whitfield preaches, do you?" Hulme answered back and said, "No, I don't but I believe that George Whitfield does."

Do you have an allegiance to the Word of God? Is it some

kind of a soul-conservation sermon? Are you in there plugging away and going through the Word of God, feeding your people week after week? You see, if you are going to have a true allegiance to God, you've got to have a true allegiance to His Word.

But second, you've got to have a true allegiance to His wisdom. You see, we have a lot of preachers who are very educated. We have a lot of preachers who have a great deal of knowledge, but there is a vast difference between knowledge and wisdom. Knowledge is what you learn by reading books and listening to tapes. Wisdom is acting on the facts, while knowledge is accumulating facts. Many of us have all the knowledge in the world and we can tell the people in the pew how to live their lives, but if we are not willing to live a godly life ourselves, then our preaching loses its power. Do you have a true allegiance to the One in authority?

When is my preaching going to become anointed? Well, it's also going to be when you take time to adore God; just to love Him and care for Him.

G. Campbell Morgan said, "There are three essentials to preaching. Truth, clarity, and passion." And on that word *passion* he gave the example of an English actor. He said a preacher once went to this actor and said, "How can you draw crowds by fiction when I am preaching truth and I'm not getting any crowd at all?" The actor turned to him and said, "Well, it's really quite simple. I present my fiction as though it were truth and you present your truth as though it were fiction."

Do you adore God in such a way that God looks at your life and says, "I've got to anoint him. I've got to bless him." Like young David who just said, "God, I'm trusting You to be to me what I've been to my flock out in the field when I face Goliath." And so when all of the negatives said, "Oh, David, don't you understand? Goliath's too big to hit." David said, "No, you don't understand. With my God, he's too big to miss."

So David went out and took five smooth stones and a sling and he brought the giant down. Not by his power. Not by his might. It wasn't a lucky shot. He adored God in such a fashion that God said, "I've got to bless his life." In other words, do people leave your church born again or bored again? Preacher, if you adore God, He's going to bless your preaching.

Finally, He's going to bless your preaching and anoint it when you are abandoned to God, when you've died to yourself, when you are really living for God. There are times when all of us must realign our hearts with God's heart. David is often called the greatest sinner in the Bible yet he's also often called the greatest saint.

Preacher, God is waiting on you to bless your ministry and to use you in such a great way and He desires to do marvelous things with your life. But will you allow Him to do it? I remember reading a quote by Charles Spurgeon when he was describing a good preacher who was a bad Christian. He said he preached so well and lived so badly that when he was in the pulpit everybody said he ought never to come out again and when he was out of the pulpit they declared he ought never to enter it again. I hope, Preacher, that doesn't describe your lifestyle. I hope you won't ever apologize for being a preacher of the gospel. It is the greatest calling which any man can ever receive. God chose you to share His Word. What a tremendous, awesome responsibility God has given to us.

Dr. B. H. Carroll, a preacher to preachers, once used the text, "I magnify mine office." He closed his message with this expression which I trust all who have the common calling of being a preacher of the Lord Jesus Christ would joyfully adopt as an individual confession. Dr. Carroll made this statement:

> I magnify mine office, O God, as I get nearer home. I can say more truthfully every year that I thank God He put me in this office. I thank Him that He would not let me have any other; that He shut me up to this glorious work. When I get home among the blessed on the bank of everlasting deliverance and I look back toward time with all of its clouds and sorrows and pains, I expect to stand up and shout for joy that down there in the fog and the mist, down there in the dust and in the struggle that God let me be a preacher. I magnify my office in life, I magnify it in death, I magnify it in heaven. I magnify it whether I am poor or rich or whether I am sick or well. Whether I am strong or weak. Anywhere, everywhere among all people. Lord God, I am glad that I am a preacher and I'm glad that I am a preacher of the glorious gospel of Jesus Christ.

Preacher, may it ever be so in your life that we, too, can stand and say that our purpose, our passion, and our power is to share the Lord Jesus Christ.

12
His Highest for My Utmost

By Joel Gregory

Joel C. Gregory

Dr. Joel C. Gregory is pastor of the Travis Avenue Baptist Church, Fort Worth, Texas. He is a "hometown boy," born in Fort Worth on April 9, 1948.

He came to Travis Avenue from his tenure as assistant professor of preaching at Southwestern Baptist Theological Seminary, Fort Worth. He taught there from 1982 to 1985. Prior to that he was pastor of Gambrell Street Baptist Church, also in Fort Worth (1977-1982).

He was married to the former Linda Mulvihill on January 22, 1968. They have two children, Grant and Garrett.

Dr. Gregory is a graduate of Baylor University (B.A., 1970, Summa cum Laude, with majors in religion and Greek); Southwestern Baptist Theological Seminary (M.Div., 1973); and Baylor University (Ph.D., 1983).

He writes extensively for magazines and journals and recently authored the study book for Southern Baptists' January Bible Study emphasis, *James: Faith Works!* With R. Earl Allen he is the co-compiler of *Southern Baptist Preaching Today* (Broadman).

Dr. Gregory is in constant demand for revivals, Bible conferences, special studies, and preaching tours.

12
His Highest for My Utmost

by Joel Gregory

Astronaut James Irwin, for whom we pray even in these days, a Christian, wrote of his experience as he looked through the window of Apollo 15. He said, "I looked back at the earth and looking at it out there in space, it appeared to me to be like a fragile, beautiful Christmas tree ornament, as if I could reach out and hold it in my very hand." Then pausing, James Irwin said, "I don't think it is blasphemous to say that that was the way the world looked to God Himself."

My assigned topic is the ascension and the present work of our Lord Jesus Christ. When we think of our Lord's ascension, invariably, correctly and usually, we think of standing there with those on the top of the Mount of Olives looking at the diminishing and disappearing form of our Lord as He ascended on high. There comes to our minds the first chapter of the Book of Acts and the ninth verse when it tells us so clearly that when He had spoken these things, while they watched He was taken up and the clouds received Him out of their sight.

I want to ask you to take another perspective with me in the simple outline of this message—not the vantage point of those disciples looking up at an ascending Lord. Instead, imagine with me the vantage point of an ascending Lord looking down at those on the Mount of Olives, looking round at the principalities and the powers and looking up at the welcome that awaited Him at the Father's right hand. You know, when He was a thousand feet up, He must have looked down and seeing that gaggle of Galileans, that den of disciples, that covey of Christians in their weakness, He must have looked at them and thought how great a task and how small they are. Perhaps He looked down at them and said, "Remember the promise of the Paraclete, remember the promise of the present." Five-thousand feet up He looked toward His right and He saw the bloody hill of Golgotha and He must have said to Himself, "Never again. Never again." He looked before Him and He saw the judgment hall of Pilate and He must have said, "Never again. Never again there." He looked to the left of Him and He saw the palace of Caiaphas the high priest, head of a prostituted religion, and He said, "Never again. Never again."

You know, twenty-five-thousand feet up He must have looked down and seen the wilderness of temptation. Seeing the wilderness of Judea, He must have said, "I have overcome the world. Never again." He looked down at Bethlehem and saw the place where He had emptied Himself and took upon Himself the form of a Servant and He said, "Never again. Never again." Then by the time He was fifty-thousand feet above the earth, He could look all the way to Nazareth and He could say, "There is where it behooved Me to be made like My brethren. But never again," said our Lord as He ascended back to the Father. That's why I have chosen the title, "His Highest for My Utmost." That's with apologies to the great devotional writer Oswald Chambers who said, "As believers we ought to give our utmost for His highest." But brothers and sisters, the only reason I can give my utmost for His highest is because an ascended, crowned Christ is there giving His highest for my utmost as a believer.

I want you to look with me at the downward look, the roundward look, and the upward look of an ascending Lord, sweeping with Him downward, then upward to the throne of God. First of all, let's look downward with our ascending Lord as He looked down at that gathering of disciples on Olivet's top. He must have thought as He looked down to them, "Remember the promise of the Paraclete and the promise of the presence." Our Lord, looking downward all the way to His ascension said, "Remember the promise of My Paraclete, My Holy Spirit with you."

That was a matter of anticipation and of realization. On the last day, the great day of the feast when our Lord Jesus Christ lifted up His voice and cried out about living water coming from within us, John wrote, "The Holy Spirit was not given because Jesus was not yet glorified." The donation of the Spirit depended upon the coronation of the King, the outpouring of the Spirit depended upon the enthroning of the Lord Jesus Christ. The Spirit is a visible vindication and a viable validation that our Lord Christ has been seated at the right hand of the Father and that He poured this out on us in His Holy Spirit.

What was first of all an anticipation became a realization in the preaching of Peter at Pentecost when he said, "Therefore being exalted to the right hand of God and having received from the Father the promise of the Holy Spirit, He poured out this which you now see and which you now hear." I don't know how it was when our Lord arrived back at the right hand of the throne of God. In some way He was greeted by the Father and the Father seated the Son but when the Father had greeted and the Son had been seated, I believe the first order of business there at the throne of heaven was as if our Lord said, "Before the twenty-four elders, bless Me. Before the living creatures, say a word. Before the myriad of angels, say, 'Worthy is the Lamb.' First, Father, I gave them the promise of the Paraclete. Send it on My church." And God opened the gates of heaven and the Holy Spirit fell on the church below.

It's His calling card. It's His identification, that donation. You may remember the name of Harry Houdini, the magician. Harry Houdini died on Halloween in 1926. Interesting timing, wasn't it? Harry Houdini was a handcuff artist, he was a self liberator, he was a spiritual investigator. Harry Houdini made a statement before he died that when he got to the other side, he was going to send back a ten-word coded message that he had left in a vault on earth. His wife, Beatrice, said she would give ten-thousand dollars to anyone who could reproduce the coded message that he would send back from the other side. And do you know what, brothers? We're still waiting.

I want to tell you, we do not worship and adore today some kind of heavenly Houdini who made a promise that He couldn't keep when He got to the right hand of the Father. He gave us the promise of the Paraclete. He kept faith in us. Our great need as we meet today is that we might know that Paraclete, the Lord Jesus who will lead us into all truth through the Spirit, that Paraclete Leader who will be our Guide, that Paraclete Reporter about whom it is said, "He will not speak of himself but He will tell us what He hears." Our great need is to be able to sing with that little prayer chorus, "Flow like a river through me. Blow like a wind upon me. Glow like a fire in me. Holy Spirit, come upon me." The downward look of the Christ said, "I give you the promise of the Paraclete."

But He also gave us the promise of the presence. Our Lord Jesus Christ said, "You'll have my Paraclete within you when I ascend." But He also said, "You will have my presence alongside of you." And that's something different. The Paraclete within and the presence alongside. Our Lord said He would be with us in the assembly of the congregation and He would be with us in the ministry of the Great Commission.

In Matthew 18:19, He gave us the standing promise that "wherever two of you are gathered together in my name, I will always be the Third and wherever three of you are gathered together, I will always be the Fourth" (author's paraphrase). In the original language of that statement it's interpreted, "I am there." The emphasis is not upon the emphatic pronoun "I." The emphasis is on the fact that He will be *there* with His people. You don't have to summon Him, send for Him, ask for Him, beg Him. He said, "If two of you are there in my name, I am there with you in the assembly of My congregation" (author's paraphrase).

Our Lord trained them by way of anticipation during those forty days between the time of His resurrection and His exalted ascension. During those forty days, John 20 says that He was among them on that first Easter and then He was gone. Then a week later on Sunday, suddenly He was among them. Gradually it began to dawn on them that whether He was there or not, when He was visible, He was no more real than when He was invisible. Whether He was not or whether He was there spiritually, He was there intermittently, sporadically, periodically. He appeared and He disappeared until finally they came to know when He's not here, He's still here. He is with us always. Then He went back to the Father.

See John the revelator there on the Isle of Patmos that jutted itself out of the water on the Aegean like a rocky fist. John, the revelator, looked over at Rome. John looked up toward heaven and said, "Where is the Lord?" And on the Lord's Day, the word came back to him, "Turn around, old man, and you will see Me. I'm where I promised to be. Right there in the midst of my churches. Walking in the midst of them, judging them, commending them, rewarding them. That is where I am."

The ascending Lord looked downward and He gave us the promise of the Paraclete. He gave us the promise of His presence, not only in the assembly of His people but in the ministry of His Great Commission. Our Lord said, "Lo, behold, I am with you all of the days. In days of bright victory and in days of bitter defeat."

The date was September 30, 1982. A friend told the story of a friend, validated by the friend's integrity that said she had a college daughter. This daughter had stayed in the library at a Texas college past the curfew time and knowing that she was going to miss the curfew, she faced the choice of going across a well-lighted pathway back the long way to the dormitory or cutting across deep, dark woods that were dangerous and were forbidden for coeds. But in her concern not to miss curfew, she went through the woods. And sure enough her greatest fear was realized. A big, ugly, threatening man jumped from behind a tree and she simply closed her eyes and said, "Jesus, Jesus, Jesus" and made her way back to the dorm.

The next morning many of the girls in the dorm were called to the police station to identify a man who had raped a girl from the dormitory that evening. They quickly identified this same man and as they were all leaving, she stayed behind and said, "I want to talk to him." For some reason the deputy let her talk to him. When she saw him she said, "That girl that you attacked was just behind me. I was in front of her. I want to ask you a question. Why her? Why not me? Why her?" And the man looked at her and said, "You've got to be kidding.

With that big guy walking alongside of you anybody would have been crazy to have bothered you."

You say, "There wasn't anybody there." Are you so sure? Our Lord giving the downward look said, "I give you the promise of the Paraclete, the promise of the presence." But the further up He went toward the throne of God, our Lord began to take the roundward look, that which was around Him as He ascended upward and onward toward the throne of God. For you see, Paul teaches us in his letters that between the brow of olives and between the throne of God, between earth below and highest heaven above our Lord had to ascend through every layer, every level, every sort of malignant, hostile, hateful spiritual force that belonged to the prince of the power of the air, the spirit that works in the children of disobedience. He faced every rank, every degree, every sort of them. In Colossians, chapter 1, Paul called them *dominions, thrones, principalities, powers*. In Romans, chapter 8, he called them *authorities*. He called them *angels*. In 1 Corinthians 15, he called these malevolent, malignant powers, *all authority, all power, all rule*. As our Lord ascended back toward heaven, He ascended through layer after layer, sphere after sphere, companies of them, legions of them, platoons of them—hateful, malignant, spiritual powers He passed through on His way to the Father's throne.

I want you to look at the roundward look with me for a moment. He swept up toward the throne of glory. It's best presented in the little letter of Colossians in chapter 2, verse 15 when we read, "And having spoiled principalities and powers, he made a shew of them openly, triumphing over them in it" (KJV). As our Lord swept up toward the throne of heaven, we read He disarmed, He displayed the principalities and the powers.

He disarmed them. It says, "having disarmed the principalities and the powers by His cross and in His ascension" (author's paraphrase). Our victorious Lord Jesus Christ disarmed, spoiled everything that can tyrannize, traumatize, paralyze, and intimidate the man or the woman of God. He spoiled them like a conquering hero going through a battlefield when His enemy had been slain and rested there lame, limp, lifeless. Our Lord on His way back to the throne of God spoiled the principalities of power, took the sting out of them once and for all for the child of God. But having disarmed them, He disgraced them. In Colossians 2:15 we read clearly He made a public *spectacle* (KJV) of them. The word means "He held them in contempt. He held them up for ridicule. He exposed them as shattered, defeated, finished in the power of His victory over sin and death and hell."

But my favorite part of this is where it says He displayed them. We are following our Lord onward and upward. As He came close to the gates of heaven, He assembled His great triumphant procession. For we read there He made a public spectacle over them, leading them in triumph into the very presence of God as defeated foes. Our Lord came to the portals of heaven, having given the downward look, having given the roundward look, disarming and disgracing everything that was a spiritual enemy to His people. He led them in *triumph* into the presence of God Himself. Do you know what that means? If you had been a Greek or a Roman, you would have known what that word means. It's only used twice in the New Testament. It means "to lead someone in a visible, open, tumultous parade of victory."

When Julius Caesar had conquered Gaul in the west and Egypt in Africa the unbelieving pagan assembled a great crowd in Rome. It was an incredible procession. People came the night before to get a seat just to see what he was going to do. First of all came the senators of Rome. Following them were those playing lewd lyrics on the lyres of Rome. Following them were those spreading perfume in the air. Following them came the booty, the spoils, the gold, the silver, the gems. Following that the conquered enemies in chains. Following that was Caesar himself. Following him came his army. It was a triumph in the city of Rome.

I want to tell you something. It was very real to those first-century Christians. Caesar had been one of the ones who crucified their Christ. Caesar was the one capturing Christians. When Paul wrote this about our ascending Lord's triumph, he wanted all the world to know that the Lord Jesus Christ entered into heaven not by the senators of Rome, but preceded by the saints of all the ages. And when our Lord Jesus Christ entered into heaven, it was a triumphant procession—not preceded by the lewd lyrics of Rome, but preceded by a heavenly anthem that came from heaven's choir itself.

When our Lord went into heaven He was not preceded by animal sacrifices but by His own blood shed for every one of us. Then came Christ at the end of that triumph. And you say, "Caesar's army followed him in Rome." Our Lord's army didn't follow Him back to the throne of God. Where is our Lord's army? Our Lord's army is here right now. When He went back to be with the church triumphant at rest, He left you and me in the church—militant until the battle is won, the day is done, and He appears the second time. Without sin and salvation we will go back for a triumphant parade. That's what our Lord did for us.

I know there are many of us with deep wounds in our lives. Pastors are under attack today—sometimes from inside their congregation, sometimes by the world, the flesh, and the devil outside. I want you to hear the word of the roundward look of the ascending Lord. He had spoiled principalities and powers. Brother Preacher, they may grab for you but if you are in Christ they can never grasp you. They may touch you but if you are in Christ they can never take you. They may try to nail you, but they can never find you if you are in the Lord Jesus Christ.

As I conclude with our Lord Jesus Christ sweeping down, up, and around, He swept up toward the very portals of heaven. I imagine it must have been something like this: angels and Old Testament saints from heaven came out to meet Him. They lined up behind Him and as they lined up behind the homecoming of the King of Kings for His coronation, those in His retinue must have cried out the words of the ancient Psalmist, "Lift up your heads, O ye gates and be ye lifted up you everlasting doors and the King of Glory shall come in." And from inside the parapets of heaven, there came back the call of the worshipping angels, "Who is the King of Glory?" And from those in His train behind Him came the call, "The Lord, strong and mighty. The Lord mighty in battle. Lift up your heads, O ye gates." And like that did our Lord go into the presence of the throne of God.

Why did He go? He took the upward look because He would receive a coronation as King and He would begin His intercession as Advocate. He would receive His coronation as King. It was prophesied in the Old Testament a thousand years before His first advent. The psalmist said, "The Lord Jehovah said to my Lord, Sit thou at my right hand until I make your enemies your footstool." What was prophesied in the Old Testament was presented in the New: the coronation of our Lord Jesus Christ. It is described in Hebrews 2. He was crowned with glory and honor. It is in Revelation 3:21, "He sits with his father in his father's throne" (author's paraphrase). Its duration is in 1 Corinthians 15 where we are told He *must* reign forever. It is a cosmic necessity. He must reign until all of His enemies are subjugated. Its dominion is in Revelation 19 where He is called King of Kings and Lord of Lords. When He went, it was for His coronation as King presented in the Old Testament and in the New.

But it was also finally to begin His intercession as Advocate. You may think all of this so far has been so much pulpit rhetoric but here it becomes pointed, personal, practical, and eternal. Because everyone of the thousands of you is just like me. You need an Advocate. I feel like Job looking up to high heaven from his ash heap. There was a Mediator to put one hand on him and another hand on me and to be our umpire, to bring us together. What Job cried for, the crowned and seated Christ answers. He is our Advocate.

In 1 John, chapter 2, one verse presents what is in the entire letter of Hebrews. "If any man sin, we have an advocate with the Father, Jesus Christ, the righteous" (v. 1). We have an Advocate presently. In the Greek New Testament that verb means "we are continuously having an advocate." Did you sin by night? You have an Advocate. Did you sin by day? You have an Advocate. Was it a sin of omission? Presently He is our Advocate. Positionally He is our Advocate. He is with the Father face to face.

One of the greatest biographies of all times is Sandberg's biography of Abraham Lincoln. In one of those many volumes he tells the story of Lincoln's little boy, Tad. Tad had a speech impediment—a cleft palate. Because of his weakness and his impediment, his father loved him all the more and would give him anything he wanted. One day a group of frontiersmen had come from Kentucky to see President Lincoln. They'd known him. He studiously avoided seeing them for a week for political reasons. He just didn't want to see them. As they were outside the grounds of the White House, they were half-cursing and saying to themselves, "Ole Abe won't see us."

Tad Lincoln heard them and said, "Would you like to see Ole Abe?" They said, "Yes." Tad said, "You can see him." He went in and said, "Papa, there are some friends of mine outside." Abraham Lincoln said, "Any friends of yours are friends of mine. Bring them in." Tad Lincoln brought in to him every one of those men that he hadn't wanted to see for a whole week. With dignity he introduced them and Abraham Lincoln took his little boy in his lap, kissed him, and said, "If they are your friends, they are my friends and they are welcome anytime."

That is a lame, tame, anemic illustration of the fact that you and I have the same difficulty. There was the holiness of God who could not receive us in our sin. There was the Son of God, whose wounds were yet visible above in beauty glorified, who said, "For My sake, Father, let them in. I am their Advocate." We need an Advocate like that. You say, "What does He argue?" I've wondered sometimes, what does the Lord say to the Father? Do you suppose He looks down and sees Joel Gregory sin a sin of commission or a sin of omission? Does He say, "Now look, Father, I want to tell you something about Ole Gregory down there. He has told a lie, he's looked where he shouldn't look, but I want you to know something. He pastors a big church. He travels around the country preaching. He's visited a lot of people in the hospital. If you put all that on one side of the scales, wouldn't it just outweigh that sin on the other side?"

You know, many people today think that's the kind of Advocate we have but thank God that's not the kind of Advocate we have. We have an Advocate who looks at the Father and says,

"You see Joel Gregory. He is a sinner. I want to tell You something. I left the crown of glory for the stable of Bethlehem for him. I emptied Myself into Bethlehem for him. I want You to know, Father, I took off My crown and put on a crown of thorns. I took off My robe and died in nakedness. I opened my veins and I shed My blood. Father, I have covered him with My doing and My dying. Forgive him because of that, Father." That is what our Advocate says.

With the downward look He gave the promise of His presence. With the roundward look He disarmed and disgraced the principalities and powers. The upward look crowned Him King, interceding as Advocate. Behind Him lay the cow stall of Bethlehem. Before Him lay the mansions of glory. Behind Him was the humiliation of mankind. Before Him was the adoration of the angels. Behind Him was death on Calvary. Before Him was a crown of glory, behind Him was the Old Jerusalem. Before Him was the New Jerusalem. "Lift up your heads, O ye gates." Lift them up and let Him reign.

13
Stargazers or Soul-winners?

By Jerry Vines

Jerry Vines

Dr. Vines has been pastor of First Baptist Church, Jacksonville, Florida since 1982. He has also served West Rome Baptist Church, Rome, Georgia, and Dauphin Way Baptist Church, Mobile, Alabama.

He is a native of Carrollton, Georgia. His wive is the former Janet Denney. They have four children: Mrs. Joy Williams, Jodi Vines, Jim Vines, and Jon Vines. He received his B.S. Degree from Mercer University, Macon, Georgia; the B.D. Degree from New Orleans Baptist Theological Seminary, New Orleans, Louisiana; and the Th.D. Degree from Luther Rice Seminary, Jacksonville, Florida.

He has authored several books: *Family Fellowship* (an exposition of 1 John); *God Speaks Today* (an exposition of 1 Corinthians); *Fire in the Pulpit; Interviews with Jesus; I Shall Return—Jesus; Great Events in the Life of Christ; A Practical Guide to Sermon Preparation;* and *Effective Guide to Sermon Delivery.*

13
Stargazers or Soul-winners?

by Jerry Vines

A number of years ago I preached a sermon from Acts, chapter 1, verses 9-12 on the subject of our Ascended Lord. In this message I would like to share with you the companion truth of this passage of Scripture, the return of our Lord and Savior, Jesus Christ.

And when he had spoken these things, while they beheld, he was taken up; and a cloud received him out of their sight. And while they looked steadfastly toward heaven as he went up, behold, two men stood by them in white apparel; Which also said, Ye men of Galilee, why stand ye gazing up into heaven? this same Jesus, which is taken up from you into heaven, shall so come in like manner as ye have seen him go into heaven. Then returned they unto Jerusalem from the mount called Olivet, which is from Jerusalem a sabbath day's journey (Acts 1:9-12).

To say good-bye to loved ones is always a difficult, moving time. In Jacksonville, Florida, where I live there is a naval base and from time to time some of our ships set sail from that port. I have seen families as they have gathered with that sailor who is getting ready to go to sea. I've seen little children as they weep with their arms around the necks of their dads. I have seen wives as they linger in their husband's embraces and I have even seen those wives run along the deck to get one final glimpse of their loved one after the ship leaves. Good-byes are always difficult times.

Saturday morning while we were getting ready to come to Atlanta, Janet, my wife, and I said goodbye to our youngest son who was going away to college and we did with him as we did with the two older children. We gathered in the kitchen and held hands together. I prayed a prayer thanking God for giving the boy to us and I gave him to God for this period of time in his life. Then I hugged his neck and told him I loved him and that I was proud of him. He hugged mine. We got in our cars and we drove away. In a little while we saw this little Toyota truck as it turned a curve up on a bridge out of sight and I said, "He's gone." When I did, my wife couldn't hold back the tears. You've never seen anything like it in your life. I got a little dust in my eyes as well. To say good-bye is always painful.

Well, it was another heartrending day on the Mount of Olives when the disciples of Jesus gathered around the Lord and said good-bye to Him as He returned to heaven. His incarnation work was ended. He had put His resurrection foot on death and He was now going back to glory which was His before the world began. And so the Bible says that Jesus Christ departed from them. Spellbound and astonished, their eyes were riveted to the skies as Jesus Christ went out of sight. As they were standing there looking at the departure of the Lord, the Bible says two men in white apparel stood by them and they said to them, "Ye men of Galilee, why stand ye gazing into heaven? This same Jesus shall so come again."

I believe those two men in white apparel were angels. I believe it because of the apparel which they wore. In the springtime some preachers get out their white suits. Well, where angels live it is always springtime, so they were clad in robes of white, beautifully symbolic of heavenly purity. I think they were also angels because of the announcement which they made. They seemed to have been the good-news angels. Maybe they were the same angels who had been one at the head and one at the foot of the place where Jesus had lain. Maybe they were those same angels who had said on that occasion to the disciples, "Why seek ye the living among the dead? He is not here. He is risen."

So I think it is fitting that those angels who advertised His birth, who attended His grave, should now announce the return of Jesus Christ from heaven again. You might very well call this scene on the Mount of Olives the first Second-Coming preaching service. All preachers who read and believe the Bible believe in the personal return of the Lord Jesus Christ.

There is an eschatalogical element in our gospel. Sooner or later the man who preaches the Bible will get around to the theme "By and by, when the morning comes. When the saints have all been gathered home." So we preach the return of our Lord. We do so because it is predicted in the Old Testament. Enoch, the seventh from Adam said, "Behold, the Lord cometh with ten thousands of his saints" (Jude 14). David, the psalmist, predicted His coming. He said, "When the Lord shall build up Zion, He shall appear in His glory" (Ps. 102:16). Daniel prophesied the return of the Lord when he said, "The Son of Man shall come in the clouds of heaven" (Dan. 7:13). Zechariah said He would come again. He said, "His feet shall stand that day upon the Mount of Olives" (Zech. 14:4).

We preach the return of our Lord because Jesus Christ

promised that He would return again. Jesus said, "If I go away, I will come again and receive you unto Myself" (John 14:4, author's paraphrase). Jesus Christ said, "Surely, I come quickly" (Rev. 22:20). Of course we preach it because it is claimed by the New Testament writers. John, the beloved disciple, said, "And now little children, let us have confidence, let us not be ashamed before him at his coming." The apostle Paul declared the return of the Lord when he said, "The Lord himself shall descend from heaven with a shout."

This passage in 1 Thessalonians is the kindergarten of the epistle. In that kindergarten, in that first epistle to believers, the apostle Paul made it very clear that we must give attention first to the truth of the return of our Lord Jesus Christ. Persons would put last what God has put first. We dare not make incidental what God has made fundamental. We must declare the return of Jesus Christ.

I want to suggest to you some of the ingredients that are involved when we gather together for a Second-Coming preaching service. Number one, a Second-Coming preaching service involves looking at a Person. The Bible says they were looking at Him. They were looking upon the Lord Jesus. The present tense of the verb indicates that it was not a fleeting glance but that it was a constant gaze. They were looking at Christ Himself. They were giving their attention to a Person.

I want to thank you, Dr. Chapman, for encouraging us and allowing us in this Pastor's Conference to spend these days focusing our attention on the Lord Jesus Christ. I'm here to tell you tonight that the Person of Jesus Christ is the sum and the substance of our Christian faith. The return and the coming of the Lord Jesus Christ is at the very center of looking at our Lord, the wonderful Savior Jesus Christ. We look at a Person tonight when we preach Jesus. The Bible says, "Sir, we would see Jesus." And the Book of Acts says Philip opened his Bible, began at the same Scripture, and preached unto him Jesus (8:35). Every time believers gather together it is another opportunity to take a look at the Person of Jesus Christ.

So these angels said, "This same Jesus." Now what I want you to do is to link that statement with Hebrews, chapter 13, verse 8 where it says, "Jesus Christ, the same yesterday, today and forever." This means that Jesus Christ dominates every dimension of time. When we preach Jesus Christ Who returns again, we are preaching One who invaded history. Jesus Christ came into history. Jesus Christ came to the datelines of all of the nations which were bent around that manger cradle. He came, stepping down from His throne to sit upon its footstool. He came, forsaking all His heavenly glory to endure earthly misery. He came to bear on His shoulders all the burdens of our sin. He came to take in His heart all the spears of pain which our sins deserved. Look at Him in His virgin birth, in His vicarious death, in His victorious resurrection. Look at Jesus Christ—the One who came, the One who saw, the One who conquered, the One who invaded history.

The One who invaded history two thousand years ago is the One Who is going to conclude history. "Of him and through him and to him are of all things" (Rom. 11:36). We are looking at a Person. Oh, I want to see Him, look upon His face. I want to praise Him for His love and grace—Jesus Christ, the same yesterday.

He is also Jesus Christ—the same today. We are looking at a Person who infuses reality. The apostle Paul beautifully prayed these words: "That Christ may dwell in your hearts by faith" (Eph. 3:17). Salvation is not only a believer being in Christ, but also Christ being in the believer. We believe that when an individual repents of personal sin and by saving faith opens his or her heart, the living Lord Jesus Christ comes walking into that one's experience and becomes real to that believer in the here and in the now.

Isn't it wonderful to know this Jesus? Isn't it wonderful to understand what reality is all about. This personal experience with the living Jesus gives meaning to our existence. He strengthens us in our times of labor. He comforts us in times of sorrow. It is a real experience with a Person. That's the Jesus I'm talking about. Jesus Christ the same yesterday—the One who invaded history. Jesus Christ the same today—the One who infuses reality. Jesus Christ the same tomorrow—the One who inhabits eternity.

Jesus is not only the personal One. Jesus Christ is not only the historical One, but Jesus Christ is the eternal One. Jesus Christ is the high and lofty One to inhabit eternity. Jesus Christ is the One who is the Father of eternity.

On April 15, 1865, Secretary of War, Edwin Stanton, rose from the bedside of Abraham Lincoln. He walked to the window, pulled the blind, looked back at the still form of Lincoln and said, "Now he belongs to the ages." Of course, that statement was only partially true because the only One who belongs to the ages is the One to whom the ages belong. I'm talking about a Person . . . the Person of Jesus Christ.

We are not so carried away with a doctrine as we are occupied with a Person. I am not so much concerned with the return of Christ as I am the Christ of the return. I'm looking for a Person. I'm looking for my Savior. When I talk about the Second Coming, I'm talking about the return of my blessed Lord.

Maybe some of you remember a few years ago when Alabama's current U.S. Senator Jeremiah Denton returned a prisoner of war from Viet Nam. It was a profound event, filled with poignant drama. You may remember that day as he stepped off the plane. There was a deep emotion and a significance about that scene that could only be comprehended by a lonely soldier and his grateful family. When the family saw him step on the ground, they did not run and kiss the nose of the plane but oh, there was a grateful little daughter who leaped to the neck of her daddy and there was a sweet wife who collapsed in the arms of her husband. They were not so much caught up with the event of his return as they were the return of a person, their father and their husband.

Ladies and gentlemen, we are talking about the return of a Person. One of these days the sky shall unfold, preparing His entrance. The stars shall applaud with thunderous praise. The sweet light on His face shall enhance those awaiting. Then we shall behold Him, face to face. That's what's involved in a Second-Coming preaching.

But then I want to say, number two, that a Second-Coming preaching service also involves listening to a promise. The words of these angels were a promise that Jesus was going to come again. "He shall come," Acts 1:11 says, "in like manner as ye have seen him go into heaven" (author's paraphrase). This lets us know that this promise is literal. The details of the return of our Lord are given in language that cannot be denied. It is couched in literal language. It is impossible to take these words in a figurative, existential sense. It is a literal event which the Bible is teaching at this point. You cannot separate the basic events of the incarnation of the Lord Jesus Christ. It all ties together. It all hangs together in one piece. If there be no literal return, there was no literal ascension. If there was no literal ascension, then there was no literal resurrection. If there was no literal resurrection, there was no literal incarnation. The whole Christian faith goes down the tubes if it's not what the Bible plainly says it's going to be.

I'll tell you what I believe. I believe that if television cameramen had been on that mountain that day, they would have seen Jesus leave from a literal mountain on a literal cloud through a literal sky in a literal body going back to a literal heaven to sit down on a literal throne. He's coming again, literally! I really believe it.

Of course this means that this is in the category of the supernatural. Now the big question today is, Is there room for the element of miracle in our universe? We must answer the question, did mankind create God or did God create mankind? Carl Sagan has said, "The cosmos is all there is and all there will ever be." But I want to tell you friends, God, the Creator, is no captive of His creation. The Bible begins, "In the beginning God created the heavens and the earth." If you can comprehend that and accept that and by faith believe that, you ought to be home free all the way through the rest of the Bible. I want to tell you, I believe that the same God who intervened in supernational incarnation will be the God Who one day will intervene in supernatural revelation. When a supernatural God gets involved, supernatural things start taking place. Clouds become vehicles, angels become taxicab drivers, and skies become skyways. He is a literal, supernatural God!

Now I want to talk about this promise. It means that He will come as the *same* Person—this *same* Jesus. You Greek scholars know that the language and the word order are in the emphatic position—This *same* Jesus. Not some other Jesus. He will not be the Jesus of world religions, sitting alongside some other dead, empty, powerless religion, but this same Jesus Who said, "I will come again." This *same* Jesus, not the Jesus of liberalism whose words are irretrievable and whose deeds are stripped of miracle, but this same Jesus Who said, "The Son of Man shall come in his glory and all of his holy angels with him."

Paul put it this way. "The Lord *Himself* shall come with a shout." I'll tell you, when He comes there'll be a *shout*. It is a word that means "a shout of command." Like a shipmaster giving a command to the rowers. It is a word like a general giving a command to his soldiers. it is like a lover calling his lover to come on up. Maybe it will be the words of Solomon when he said, "The voice of my beloved! Behold, he cometh leaping upon the mountains, skipping upon the hills. . . . 'Rise up, my love, my fair one, and come away'" (Song of Sol. 2:8, 10, KJV).

Maybe it will be the words of John on the Isle of Patmos when he heard in Revelation 4:1 "a voice like a trumpet from heaven saying, Come up hither and I will show you things which must take place hereafter" (author's paraphrase). I'll tell you, He is going to come as the same Person, He is going to come for the same people. It was the disciples who were gathered there. No unbelievers were there. Only born-again, blood-washed believers were on the mountain that day. He's coming for the same people.

Now imagine with me for a moment a great heap of metals scattered over the ground. Some are on top of the ground and some are under the ground. They are metals of all sorts. There are copper, zinc, iron, gold, and brass. Then suppose a big magnet is lowered over that field and then suddenly from under the ground and on top of the ground pieces of iron leap to the magnet as it is lord. Only the iron is taken. Why are none of the other metals disturbed? It is because only the iron has the nature of the magnet. One of these days the Lord Jesus is going to nod to the angel Gabriel. Gabriel will reach for the trumpet of God from the shimmering walls of the heavenly city. Gabriel will blow that trumpet to wake the living dead and the Lord Jesus will swoop down the stairway of the skies. Everybody on this earth and under the earth who has the divine nature of Christ in them, all of those who are heaven born will be heaven bound. They will be caught up out of this world to go home to be with the Lord.

Friend, if you're a Christian, you've got one of two experiences waiting for you. If you die before Jesus comes again, it'll be resurrection. The dead in Christ shall rise first, and wherever death overtook your body, you shall come forth. Maybe you fell in a jungle somewhere and the bones of your flesh have been picked by birds. Maybe you fell into the churning, belching sea and that is where your body remains. Maybe you'll be buried in a little country cemetery somewhere but, ah, when that shout . . . listen, do you know what? Three times in the Bible Jesus shouted and every time a resurrection occurred. He shouted before the tomb of Lazarus, "Lazarus, come forth," and a man came forth. He shouted on the cross and the saints came out of their graves. He'll shout in the sky one of these days and millions will come forth in resurrection glory. Oh, what a resurrection! But you may be living . . . you may be alive. If so, it is going to be rapture for you. "We which are alive and remain shall be caught up together in the clouds, to meet the Lord in the air" (1 Thess. 4:17).

When I was a pastor in Rome, Georgia, a congregation in our town was building a new church and they put a sign out on the top where they were building their church. I will never forget it. It announced the name of the church, then on top of the sign here's what it said: "Rapture Preparation Center. Get right for the flight." I like that. Did you know there is going to be a glorious duet sung when the Lord comes for His own? Over in 1 Corinthians we are told the lyrics of that beautiful duet. It says this: "O death, where is thy sting? O grave, where is thy victory?" If you are a dead believer and you are resurrected, I can see you now going up and looking back at old grim death and saying, "Ha, Ha, you couldn't sting me, could you, Death?" If you are dead when the Lord comes, you'll look back at that grave and you'll say, "You couldn't hold me, could you?"

I don't know which I'll be, whether I'll be dead or whether I'll be alive, so I've just learned both parts of the duet and I'm going to be prepared when He comes. He'll catch us up, He'll take us up to the Judgment Seat and clean us up and then He'll take us to the Marriage Supper and He'll cheer us up and we'll have a honeymoon with Jesus for a thousand years. He's coming again. "When He comes, our glorious King, all His ransomed home to bring. Then anew this song we'll sing, Hallelujah, what a Savior."

He is coming as the same Person, He is coming for the same people and He is coming to the same place. Zechariah said, "And his feet shall stand in that day upon the Mount of Olives. And the Mount of Olives shall cleave in the midst thereof" (14:4).

The return of Richard the Lionhearted was one of the thrilling epochs of the English people. All of England loved Richard. He was a great leader of men. He was a wrestler, a runner, a poet, and a general. While Richard was away in the Crusades, his kingdom fell on hard times. His wicked brother, John, sought to capture the throne. John was a selfish, cruel, wicked man. The people suffered, and they longed for Richard's return.

Well, one day Richard returned. He landed on the shores of

England and marched straight for his throne. The castles of John tumbled like bowling pens. None dared stand in his place and he marched straight to his throne, there to reign again. The bells of London rang, the people shouted, "The Lion is back. Long live the king."

Praise God that one of these days a king greater than Richard is coming back to recover a greater domain than England. You can read about it. It's over in the Book of the Revelation and in the nineteenth chapter, here's what it says, "And I saw heaven open and behold a white horse and he that sat upon him was called faithful and true." Let me skip. ". . . and the armies which were in heaven followed him upon white horses clothed in white linen and out of his mouth goeth a sharp sword, that with it he should smite the nations" (19:11,14,16). Let me skip again. ". . . he hath on his vesture and on his thigh a name written, KING OF KINGS AND LORD OF LORDS."

He'll come down from the sky. His feet will stand on the Mount of Olives. This world will turn to a garden of roses underneath His feet. He will march down the slopes of Olivet. He'll put all of those right who have mismanaged His world. He'll march up through the Eastern Gate. He'll go right on into the city of Jerusalem and He'll sit down on the throne of His father, David, and He'll rule and reign.

You say, "Preacher, I think that's going to be a spiritual event." Let me read Luke, chapter 1. The announcement of Gabriel to Mary says, "And behold thou shalt conceive in thy womb." That happened literally, didn't it? ". . . and shall bring forth a son." That happened literally, didn't it? ". . . and shall call His Name Jesus." That happened literally, didn't it? ". . . and He shall be great." That was literally true. ". . .and shall be called the Son of the Highest." That was literally true, wasn't it? ". . . and the Lord God shall give unto Him the throne of His Father, David."

Now beloved, by what kind of hermeneutical gymnastics can you make the first part of that verse spiritual and the second part literal? Listen, friend, the only throne David ever had was an earthly throne and Jesus is going to rule and reign on this earth for a thousand years.

A few days ago somebody said to me, "Have you ever been to Jerusalem?" I said, "Oh, yes, I've been a few times." They said, "Well, do you think you'll ever go back now with all of this terrorist activity going on?" I said, "Oh, yes, I'll be back. One fair morning I'll wake up in the city of Jerusalem and I'll go walking down the streets and I'll walk up on a woman who has a wagonload of roses. I'll reach over there to get me some of those roses and I'll discover there are no thorns on those roses. I'll says, "Ma'am, where in the world did you get those roses?" She will say, "Oh, I've grown them out there in the desert." I'll say, "In the desert?" She'll say, 'Yes, haven't you heard? The Lord reigns in Zion and the desert shall rejoice and blossom as a rose."

I'll walk a little bit further. I'll go into the mall and I'll go to the pet shop and I'll hear a man saying, "I'd like to buy that cobra there for my baby boy." I will say, "Sir, what in the world are you doing buying a snake for your boy?" And he'll say, "Didn't you know the Lord reigns in Zion and the lion shall eat straw like the ox and the suckling child shall play upon the hole of the asp" (see Isa. 11:7-8). I'll go a little further and I'll say, "Where are your police departments?" They will say, "We don't have any." "Where are your soldiers?" "We don't have any." "Where are your military academies?" "We don't have any of those here. The Lord reigns in Zion." "They have beat their swords into plowshares and their spears into pruning hooks and nations have learned war no more" (see Isa. 2:4).

I'll go a little bit further and I'll say, "I want to visit your hospitals. I want to encourage some of your cancer patients." They will say, "We don't have any cancer patients here." I'll say, "You don't?" "No, no, no. Not since the Lord reigns in Zion. The inhabitants in this land never say, 'I'm sick.'" I'll say, "What about your homes for the crippled children?" "We don't have any. The Lord reigns in Zion and the lame shall leap in that day." "Well, what about the home for your deaf and dumb?" "There are not any of those either. The tongue of the dumb shall sing on that day and the ears of the deaf shall be unstopped in that day. The Lord reigns in Zion." And I'll say, "Well, what about your funeral homes and what about your cemeteries?" They will say, "There aren't any of those. The Lord reigns in Zion." And I'll say, "Where do you folks go to church?" And they'll say, "We all go up to Jerusalem to worship the great King." And I'll look up there and I'll see the Lord high and lifted up and I'll hear the great choir as they sing, "O hail the power of Jesus' Name; let angels prostrate fall. Bring forth the royal diadem and crown Him Lord of all." What a promise!

A Second-Coming service not only involves looking at a Person and listening to a promise but, number three, it also involves leaving with a purpose. These disciples were absolutely transfixed. They were looking their eyes out. They were motionless by the vision and then in that moment the angel said to them, "The Lord is going to come again." And they leaped down from that mountain. Their hearts were pounding with exhilaration. Their steps were fast. Now they had a purpose. Now they had a reason.

When you go to a Second-Coming service, it does not exist in and of itself. There is a purpose to talking about the Second Coming of Jesus Christ. It brings us to the subject of worship. If Jesus Christ is not coming again, then musicians must lay aside their instruments. Singers must still their voices. Preachers must fold their Bible. If Jesus is not coming again, there is no reason for us to worship. But if Jesus is going to come again, then let the worship begin.

Well, what shall be our Call to Worship, preacher? "Not forsaking the assemblying of ourselves together but so much the more and exhorting one another as the matter some is as ye see the day approaching" (Heb. 10:25). Well, how shall we pray in our worship service? We shall pray, "Thy kingdom come, thy will be done." What will the choir sing in the service? They'll sing that some golden daybreak Jesus shall come, and battles will all be won. They'll sing that He'll shout the victory, and break through the blue for me and for you.

Can you have the Lord's Supper at the Second-Coming service? Sure you can. "For as often as ye eat this fruit and drink this cup, you do show the Lord's death 'til He comes." Well, do you have any word for me to give my fellow believers as we leave the service? Oh, yes. Just whisper in their ear, "Maranatha, the Lord cometh."

It was a great day for Scotland when John Knox came to preach. He'd come to the edge of the village and he'd say to the first farmer he found, "Tell all of your neighbors I'm going to be preaching at the meeting house at early candlelight." That farmer, in his joy, would scramble to the top of his house. He'd put his hands to his face and he'd say, "Neighbors, neighbors, Knox is coming. Meeting in the meeting house at early candlelight." Two or three more would scramble to the roofs of their houses and pretty soon there would be singing and shouting all over the valley, "Knox is coming, Knox is coming." Oh Lord Jesus, how long, how long before we shout the glad song, that You are returning? Hallelujah! Christ returns! Amen!

But the Lord's coming is also a call for us to leave this service to witness. "Why stand ye gazing," said the angels? Now some people have a tendency to make stargazers out of those of us who believe the Lord *is* coming. They say, "You folks who believe in the literal return of the Lord are so heavenly minded that you are no earthly good." Of course, I recognize there may be an element of truth in that charge. Some have presumed upon this truth. There have been those in past history who have suspended activity and climbed a hill somewhere.

I read about one group that got all their horses and some fodder upon the hill. They put on white robes. The women sewed ascension robes so they could go up in modesty. They waited and they waited but He didn't come. Red-faced they slunk back down the side of the hill. I want to tell you something. This Second Coming is no call to be a stargazer. Jesus said, "It is not for you to know the time or the season which the Father has put in his own power."

Listen, friend. I'm not God. I don't even try to be Assistant God. I don't know when Jesus is going to come. I tell you what though. If I were God and some screwball accidently predicted the day the Lord was going to come, I'd change it to mess him up. But that's not for you to know. That's the Father's power. "Ye shall receive power and ye shall be witnesses unto me." The truth of the Second Coming ought to make soul-winners out of us. Sure, study the signs of the times, but don't forget the sighs of the times of those with hungry hearts. Of course, ride the four horses of the Apocalypse but don't fail to ride your small compact cars out into the highways and the hedges and win souls to Jesus. Tickle the ten toes of Daniel, but use the toes you've got to get out there and tell people about the Lord Jesus Christ.

It's a call to witness for the Lord. I'll tell you something else. It's a call to wait. The Bible says, "From whence we look for our Savior, the Lord Jesus." The Bible says we should live soberly, righteously, Godly in this present world. We are to live looking for the return of our Lord. If we really believe Jesus is coming again, it is an incentive to intensify our work for the Lord. Waiting times are not wasted times. "We'll work 'til Jesus comes and we'll be gathered home."

I'll tell you something else. It's a call to purity in the Christian life. "Every man that hath this hope in him purifies himself even as he is pure." I have a feeling that the reason we are battling such worldliness in our Southern Baptist churches is that the truth of the imminent return of our Lord Jesus is flickering very low in the hearts of Southern Baptist people.

The wedding is over. The cake has been cut, the rice has been thrown. Kathy and Tom are finally in the car alone. As they drive away amidst the chorus of well-wishers, Kathy moves away from Tom and she says, "Tom, take me home." And he says, "Home? Why Kathy, you know our home won't be ready for two weeks. Now we are going on our honeymoon." "Oh, no, Tom. I don't mean your home. I mean my home. My mother's home. Tom, I really do love you and I have taken you as my husband but you don't expect me to change my life, do you? I'll try to see you once a week if it's convenient. And when I'm sick, I'll expect you to come. And when I run out of money, Tom, I'll expect you to provide it and if there is something I can't handle, I'll expect you to help me out. But in the meantime, hands off my life."

Ladies and gentlemen, I say to you tonight, that wouldn't be a marriage. That would be a mockery. Yet there are thousands of people who say to the Lord Jesus, "Jesus, thank You for loving me. I accept You as my Savior. If it's convenient and if I'm sick, I'll expect You to heal me. And if I'm out of money, I'll expect You to provide some money but Jesus, You don't expect me to change my life, do You? Hands off my life!"

Oh dear friends, the Bible warns we should be very careful that we not be shamed before Him at His coming. I have a feeling if our Southern Baptist people believed in the return of Jesus the way we ought to, some of them would get that beer out of the refrigerator. I have a feeling if some Baptist preachers really believed the Second Coming they preach, they'd yank that cable channel off their television sets. I don't know about you, but I want to so live that when He comes I nor He will be embarrassed.

I used to hear R. G. Lee tell about Jamey Sotter, the town cynic. R. G. Lee used to tell about how ole Jamey Sotter used to wear crepe on his hat. When he came to die, his pastor was there and Jamey said, "Pastor, when I die I want you to take the crepe from around my hat and throw it in the fire. I'm not going to need it in the land to which I'm going." Then he said, "Forty-four years ago I loved a girl and she loved me, crippled though I am. Everyday we used to meet one another where the roses bloom. It was so sweet. Then one day I went to meet her and she didn't come. Great anguish filled my heart. I went back the next day and I saw her brother coming and I knew something was wrong. He told me that she had died. For forty-four years now I've worn this crepe in my hat."

Then as if he could see out into eternity, his old, rugged face brightened with a light from heaven and he reached out his hands as if he could see the girl he'd loved and lost forty-four years before and he said, "Mamie, I have kept the tryst."

When that day comes, I want to be able to say, "Jesus, I've kept the faith." Jesus is coming. Oh, Jesus is coming again. My heart is so happy. My soul is so glad—for Jesus is coming again!

14
Crown Him Lord

By Eugene Ridley

Eugene Ridley

Eugene Ridley, native of Jackson County, North Carolina, has recently become pastor of Pine Valley Baptist Church, Wilmington, North Carolina. Previously he was an evangelist and pastored several churches in western North Carolina. He is a graduate of Fruitland Baptist Bible Institute, Hendersonville, North Carolina, and attended Luther Rice Seminary, Jacksonville, Florida. Besides his native state, he has preached revivals and taught Bible conferences in several states and foreign countries. He is married to the former Gloria O'Dear and they have a son, Stephen.

14
Crown Him Lord

by Eugene Ridley

Colossians 1:14-22:

In whom we have redemption, through his blood, even the forgiveness of sins. Who is the image of the invisible God, the firstborn of every creature, for by him were all things created, that are in heaven, and that are in earth, visible and invisible, whether they be thrones, or dominions, or principalities, or powers: all things were created by him and for him. And he is before all things, and by him all things consist. And he is the head of the body, the church: who is the beginning, the firstborn from the dead, that in all things he might have the preeminence. For it pleased the Father that in him should all fullness dwell. And having made peace through the blood of his cross by him to reconcile all things unto himself; by him, I say, whether they be things in earth, or things in heaven. And you, that were sometime alienated and enemies in your mind by wicked works, yet now hath he reconciled in the body of his flesh through death, to present you holy and unblameable and unreprovable in his sight.

Aren't you glad for what God did in Christ on Calvary that purchased your salvation? Salvation is of the Lord. Salvation is by the Lord. "For by grace are ye saved through faith: and that not of yourselves. It is the gift of God, not of works, lest any man should boast" (Eph. 2:8-9). I was thrilled just listening to that beautiful hymn the other day which says: "All hail the power of Jesus' name, Let angels prostrate fall; Bring forth the royal diadem and crown him Lord of all."

I want to speak this evening on crowning Him Lord. You do not make Him something. He already is. He is already Lord, but within your life you crown Him Lord. Crown Him Lord, based on this Scripture this evening. Crown Him Lord because of redemption. He does redeem. Crown Him Lord because of revelation. He does reveal. Crown Him Lord because of reconciliation. He has reconciled persons unto God. Verse 14 teaches us that we need to crown Jesus Lord, first of all because of redemption. Notice those marvelous, majestic, mighty words when Paul wrote, "In whom we have redemption." Here's the route of it—"through His blood."

Now here are the results—"even the forgiveness of sin." I believe you will agree with me that Jesus needs to be crowned Lord. And I believe that you will agree that we need to crown Him Lord because of redemption, for He did what none other could do. He redeemed us and wrote our names in the Lamb's Book of Life. We are blood-washed children of God. We've been made heirs of God, joint heirs of God with Jesus, and we're here to crown Him Lord because of redemption.

First of all, the route of redemption is "through His blood." There is no other way of salvation except through what God did in Christ on Calvary. That's where your salvation and my salvation were purchased. Now, if you agree with me, I want you to respond at this time. Does the Bible say something similar to this in the Old Testament? Does the Bible say the soul that sins shall surely die? Does the Bible say something close to that? Does the Bible, then, in the New Testament, say that the soul that sins shall die and all "have sinned and come short of the glory of God?" Does the same Bible also say "the wages of sin is death?" Does the Bible say that? Well, if that be true, and—there are no ifs about it—that is true, then God said the soul that sins has to die. "All have sinned and come short of the glory of God," and "the wages of sin is death." Within myself, I am hopeless, helpless, doomed, damned, depraved, without hope, without help in this world. Within myself, without anything intervening within myself, I have no way out, if that be true. And it *is* true.

Then you say, "Well, how, then, can God, who can't lie; how can God, who is true, how can God then keep His word, put me to death, and let me live at the same time? How, under God's heaven, can a person be put to death and live at the same time?" There is but one way—to be put to death in the One that came back to life again on that third day. How can God, who must keep His word, put me to death and let me live at the same time? God said, "Gene Ridley, if you sin, you have to die. Gene Ridley, you have sinned, you are going to die, but there is one hope for you, Gene Ridley, and that's to put you to death in My Son."

Do you know how you were saved? The Bibles teaches, "He, God the Father, hath made Him, God the Son, who knew no sin to become sin, that we might be made the righteousness of God in Him." Two thousand years ago, God the Father reached down and picked up Gene Ridley and all of my sins and laid me over on Christ Jesus. God picked you up with all of your sins and laid you over on Christ Jesus. That day God the Father looked down at the old, rugged cross, and that Man hanging on the cross. That Man was guilty of every sin that had ever been committed on the face of God's earth. And God said, "That does not look like My Son. My Son never lied; that Man lied. My Son never committed murder; that Man is guilty of murder." That day God the Father looked down and saw Gene Ridley, instead of seeing Jesus Christ. God said that if Gene Ridley sinned, he had to die. God put Gene Ridley to death in Jesus Christ. I got into Jesus, and Jesus died.

In 1968, Robert Clegg led me to Jesus in the First Baptist Church of Sylva, North Carolina. I identified, and I said, "All right, God, if I have to die, one way or another, I have to die. And I know if I die within myself, I'll go to hell, but if I die in Jesus, I'll go to heaven. I choose Your route, God." So I laid back in Christ Jesus. Two thousand years ago, Gene Ridley got into Jesus and Jesus died. But in 1968 Jesus got into Gene Ridley, and—hallelujah!—I get to live! I got into Him; He died. He got into me, I get to live.

Paul got a glimpse of that when he said, "I live; nevertheless, not I but Christ liveth within me" (Gal. 2:20). God the Father looked down that day and saw me; Jesus died. God the Father looks down tonight at the pulpit in Atlanta, Georgia, and He looks through the blood of His darling, righteous Son, and He sees righteousness, holiness, and purity. He says, "That old boy doesn't look like Gene Ridley, that looks like My Son, Jesus," and I get to live. Hallelujah, what a Savior!

Do you know how you were saved? You were saved by what God did in Christ on Calvary. That's how you were saved. Do you know why you were lost? You were lost like Mephibosheth. The only sin Mephibosheth was guilty of was being kin to the wrong person. He was under the death warrant because he had the wrong blood running through his veins. And David sent to Lodebar after him for Jonathan's sake. David said to Mephibosheth: "I'm going to make you as one of my kids. It's just going to be like you had been born again, Mephibosheth, into my family." You know what was wrong with me? I was kin to the wrong person. Do you know whose blood flows through our veins? Adam's.

Do you know why we act like Adam? He's our Daddy. Do you know why you act like your Daddy? You have his blood running through your veins. Do you know the reason Gene Ridley acts like Claude Ridley? I have Claude Ridley's blood in my veins. Do you know the reason Stephen Ridley acts like Gene Ridley? He has my blood in his veins. That's the reason Jesus said to Nicodemus, "Nicodemus, if it were possible, it would be better if you could just take the blood out of your veins, and just become born again, and be somebody else." That's what He said. "Nicodemus, you are just kin to the wrong person. That's all of your problem. Nicodemus, you're kin to Adam."

Romans says, "By the first Adam, man was plunged into depravity. But by the second Adam, we've been delivered unto God" (author's paraphrase). Through the blood of the first Adam, we were condemned, but through the Second Adam's blood, we've been cleansed. God placed the first Adam in a sleep, took from his side a rib, and made his bride Eve. The Second Adam hung on Calvary's tree. His heart exploded, the blood and fluid ran down His side, a soldier took a spear and pierced His side, and out flowed the blood and the water. From the Second Adam's side came His bride, the church of the living God.

The only way to live is to die in Christ Jesus. The only way to live forever is to die in Christ Jesus, for Christ Jesus' righteousness is applied to us. When our sins had been applied to Him, he died. But when His righteousness is applied to us, we get to live. Hallelujah, what a Savior! Thank God, and crown Him Lord for redemption. Any way other than that will not get you saved. There's but one route of salvation, and that's through the blood of the Son of God. Somewhere along the line, you have to get into Him, and somewhere along the line, He has to get into you. When you got into Him, He died; but when He gets into you, you live. That is the plan of salvation. That's the reason you'll have to say it's "by grace you are saved through faith, and that not of yourselves. It is the gift of God, not of works, lest any man should boast" (Eph. 2:8-9, author's paraphrase).

Not only do I want you to see the route of redemption, but I want you to see the results of redemption. Notice Colossians 1:14: "In whom we have redemption, through his blood, even the forgiveness of sins." Not only the route of redemption, but the result of redemption. Because Jesus Christ has redeemed us, we have been forgiven our sins.

I went back to a department store in my home town a few years and was buying a coat off the clothes rack, when a lady walked up to me and I recognized her as one of my high-school teachers. She said to me, "Are you Gene Ridley?"

I said, "Yes, Ma'am."

She said, "They tell me you're making a preacher."

I said, "I am."

"Are you still preaching?"

They always say *still*. They expect me to cash it in anytime. I said, "Yeah, I'm still preaching."

"Well, I'd never thought you'd have been a preacher. I remember what you used to be."

And I thought, *Old gal, you'd better be proud of yourself. You can do something God can't do.*

I want to tell you something. Crown Him Lord, because of *redemption*. He saved you. The route of it is His blood. The results—the forgiveness of sin. Aren't you glad you don't have to walk around under the guilt of all that sin? That He saved you and washed you clean in the blood of the Lamb?

Crown Him Lord not only because of redemption, but because of revelation. Look at verse 15. You didn't discover anything about God. Everything you know about God has been revealed. Verse 1 says, "Who is the image of the invisible God, the firstborn of every creature." "It's Jesus Christ, and we need to crown Him because of revelation.

First of all, because He reveals the person of God. Do you know who Jesus was, when He was curled as a five-minute-old baby in the arms of His mama? They looked down in His face, and said, "His name shall be called Emmanuel," because God is *with us*. The Bible says "In him dwelt the fullness of the Godhead bodily." In other words, in one body dwelt all of God. Jesus said, "When you've seen Me, you've seen the Father. I and My Father are one." The Bible says that God was in Christ reconciling the world unto Himself. Jesus Christ is not part God and part man. Jesus is 100 percent God and 100 percent man. He's the *God-man!*

Do you know who Jesus is? He's God in the flesh, not part God. Sure He's prophet, sure He's priest, sure He'll be king, but He's *all God*, not part of God. Before the mount of transfiguration, His disciples had seen Him as the Son of God, but on that day they saw Him as God the Son. God Who was on the inside came outside. John 1 says, "In the beginning was the Word, and the Word was with God, and the Word was God, and the Word was made flesh and dwelt among us, and we beheld His glory as the glory of the only begotten Father full of grace and truth." Jesus Christ has always been God and He'll always be God. There has never been a time He wasn't God; there will never be a time He won't be God. Before everything was, He was; after everything's gone, He's still going to be. He said, "I am the Alpha, I am the Omega, I am He that was, is, and is to come, the Almighty." Jesus Christ said, "Before Abraham was, I was." Jesus Christ has always been who He said He was—God, Almighty God.

Now he hasn't always been human, but He's always been God. The Bible says that He was made a body. He had a body prepared for Him. He left heaven without a body, and went back to heaven with a body. That's the reason behind the kenosis passage of Scripture, which says, "Let this mind be in you," and goes on to say that God hath given Him a name which is above every name. At the name of Jesus, everything will bow. Now God was saying: you've always bowed to Him as the Word. He's always been God, and there never has been a time when He has not been God. Things in heaven have bowed to Him because He's God; things on earth have bowed to Him because He's God. Now just because He's come back here with an earthly body—physical body—doesn't mean He's any less God. His earthly name is Jesus, but this is the same Word that left here, headed toward Bethlehem that day, and was vehicled into the world through the womb of a virgin. This is still the same God. You still must bow to Him. We still bow to Him.

Crown Him Lord because of redemption—the route of it, the results of it. Crown Him Lord because of *revelation*, because He's God in the flesh. He was God in Bethlehem. He was God when He was toddling around as a three-year-old. He was God at the bar-mitzvah service where you saw Him when He was twelve years old. Then there were eighteen dark years. Finally you saw Him at the baptismal service. He walked seventy-five miles to be baptized, He who didn't even *need* to be baptized. Now you vote against baptism. Amen!

Old John the Baptist was out there baptizing those old boys, many of them herdsmen. I mean he set all the associational records and had all the preachers jealous of him, you know. Baptizing those old boys, he'd say, "I'm going to baptize you with water. But there's One coming who is going to baptize you with fire. There's One coming and when He gets here, I've got to decrease, He's got to increase. There's One coming, and I'm not even worthy to touch the latches on His sandals." All of a sudden, after he'd baptized that old boy by immersion, he looked and said, "Behold! Yonder He is. Behold the Lamb of God, that takes away the sin of the world."

He's always been God, He'll always be God. Jesus Christ reveals the person of God. I take issue with this outfit that sees God in Creation. It's a fallen creation at its best. You say, "Can I see God?" You might see His handiwork, but the only way you'll ever get a twenty-twenty, clear-cut vision of Almighty God is to look at Jesus from the cradle to the cross. You look at Jesus in any situation, and you get a twenty-twenty, clear-cut picture of Almighty God. He's God.

Not only do you crown Him Lord because of revelation, because He reveals the person of God, but in Colossians 1:16, He reveals the *power* of God.

> For by Him were all things created, that are in heaven, and that are in earth, visible and invisible. Whether they be thrones, or dominions, or principalities, or powers: all things were created by Him, and for Him. And He is before all things, and by Him all things consist.

Jesus Christ reveals the power of God. He spoke this world into creation.

I wonder what went through the mind of little Jesus, because He's always been God. I wonder. When Joseph would come home from the carpentry shop, and Mary said, "Oh, Joseph, do you realize Jesus spoke His first words today?" Do you ever imagine what went through the mind of little Jesus? "Oh Mama, I spoke one time and the world came into existence." I know He didn't choose to start His ministry until around the age of thirty, but He could have walked on the water at three days old. He is God. He is God, and He revealed the power of God. Thank God for the revelation of the power of God. And He holds everything together.

Not only do you need to crown Him Lord because of redemption, the route, the results. Not only do you need to crown Him Lord because of revelation, because He reveals the person and the power of God, but we need to crown Him Lord because of *reconciliation*. Notice, please, verse 20. "And having made peace through the blood of His cross, by Him to reconcile all things unto Himself; by Him, I say, whether they be things in earth, or things in heaven."

The Bible says God was in Him *reconciling* the world unto Himself. Do you realize the only reason earth and heaven have ever been reconciled? Jesus Christ was hanging between heaven and earth as if neither wanted Him, but hanging there He took all the sins of this world upon Himself. Finally, after all the other attempts by mankind had failed, Jesus Christ hanging between heaven and earth, God's only Son, finally reconciled earth and heaven. Thank God for reconciliation.

Reconciliation first of all brings peace. He said we will have peace because we've been reconciled to God. We're no longer at war with God. We have peace between us, we have peace with God—the peace of God—and it's all because of what God did in Christ on Calvary.

Not only do we have peace through reconciliation, we have presentation through reconciliation. Notice what it says in verses 21 and 22.

And you, that were sometimes alienated and enemies in your mind by wicked works, yet now hath He reconciled in the body of His flesh through death, to present you holy and unblameable and unreprovable in His sight.

You are reconciled to God the Father.

Crown Him Lord—*redemption*. Crown Him Lord—*revelation*. Crown Him Lord—*reconciliation*. Because of peace and presentation.

Here is a personal illustration. A little over nineteen years ago in Sylva, North Carolina, I started dating a young lady by the name of Gloria Jean O'Dear. I didn't tell my Mama and Daddy who I dated for several reasons, you know. I didn't figure it was anybody's business, didn't tell anybody who I dated. But one day, on Christmas Eve nineteen years ago, I went across the river to the old home place, and I said to my Dad, "Daddy, would you mind me bringing a friend tomorrow, to eat Christmas dinner with us?"

Daddy said, "Why Gene?"

I said, "Well, I just want to."

And Daddy said, "Well, who is it?"

And I said, "Well . . . ," and I told him who it was.

He said, "Well, why?"

And I said, "Well, I just want to."

"Well," he said, "You never brought a girl home before."

And I said, "Well, Daddy, if you must know, I've asked this one to be my bride. I'd like to bring her home to present her to you and Mama."

The next day I got up and drove twelve miles or more, to her home. When she came through that door, I've never seen her more beautiful in all my life. Every hair was in place—I don't believe she even put her head on a pillow the night before. We got in my car, drove down to my house, drove up that drive-way, went up to the door that swung open, and my Dad, who had never greeted me before, was there. He said, "Come on in, Son." We went on in and I introduced her.

We'd always had great Christmas dinners, but we had never seen such a Christmas dinner like this one. There were even fancy dishes and glasses on the table that Mom said were just to look at. They were honoring Gloria Jean O'Dear. Now, had she just come in off the street, they would have been nice to her, but they wouldn't have treated her like royalty as they did that day. They wouldn't have greeted her royally. That day they greeted her because she was with their baby boy. They honored her because of their son.

I want to tell you something. Jesus Christ left Heaven's glory one day, came to earth's gloom, sought me out, chose me, and I answered and said, "Yes, I will." An experience took place. Jesus Christ said, "Yes, I will." Jesus Christ said, "Now, Gene, one of these days I'm going to take you and present you to the Father in glory." I want to tell you something—I'm part of the bride of Christ. And when He splits that eastern sky and calls me home to the Marriage Supper of the Lamb, you've never seen such a table prepared, and I'll sit there for about seven years, if my calculations are right. There to be presented before God because of nothing I've done, but to God be the glory for what He has done. Crown Him Lord, because He *redeems* you. Crown Him Lord, because He *revealed* God the Father. Crown Him Lord, because He's *reconciled* you, has given you peace, and one day is going to present you to God the Father. God bless you.